NFTs: A Beginner's Guide

A crypto ART and its new trend online

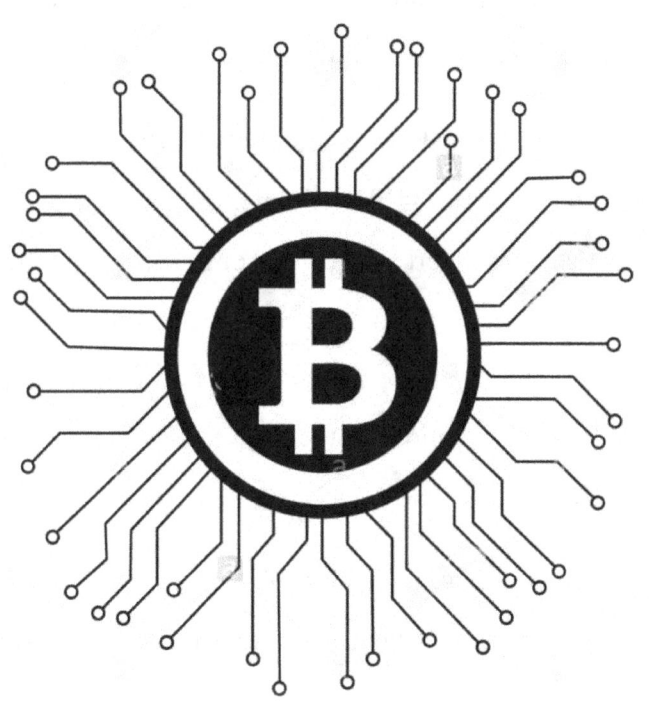

INTRODUCTION

Since the marvels of Satoshi Nakamoto ushered in Bitcoin, the world's first successful blockchain network, things have never been the same again. This digital revolution has created a multi-trillion-dollar virtual infrastructure. Currencies, borderless assets, non-bank loans, and boundless arts interact in a seemingly endless river of prosperity.

And when we talk about boundless arts, non-fungible tokens (NFTs) come to mind. While NFTs brought artists onto the blockchain platform, NFTs are not a preserve of artists. Newer applications and use-cases are coming up.

While this book is primarily focused on NFTs, this also book introduces you to the world of blockchain and cryptocurrencies. It is through blockchain networks that it becomes possible to create NFTs. Blockchain is the mother of NFTs. And it is through cryptocurrencies that NFT creation gets funded. Thus, understanding blockchain and cryptocurrency is a prerequisite to understanding NFT.

If you are already familiar with blockchain and cryptocurrency, then brushing up your knowledge causes no harm. But, if you need not repeat the lessons, you can skip Part I and go straight to Part II of this book, where NFTs are introduced and explained in detail.

This book has a simple approach to enable you to get the basics of NFTs. Above all, explore other NFT use-cases beyond the arts. NFT is not just for artists, even though it is artists who molded it. It is also for traders, investors, financiers, and so many other kinds of specialists. Information provided herein is enough to arouse the creative genius within you. You have a stake in NFT. Don't lose the chance. Blockchain network is the place to farm your ideas, bake your dreams and mint your fortunes.

Table Of Contents

Part I 1

BLOCKCHAIN - THE NFTs BACKBONE . 1

   Chapter 1 2

   Understanding Blockchain Technology 2

   Chapter 2 34

   Blockchain Applications and Use-Cases 34

   Chapter 3 89

   Cryptocurrency – The NFTs Power Coins 89

PART II 116

INTRODUCTION TO NFTs 116

   Chapter 4 117

   The Nature of NFTs 117

   Chapter 5 129

   What Do You Have that You Can Turn into Your Own NFT? 129

   Chapter 6 142

   How to Create Your NFT 142

PART III 148

MAKING MONEY FROM NFTS 148

   Chapter 7 150

   How to Monetize Your NFT 150

   Chapter 8 161

   Trading in NFTs 161

   Chapter 9 199

   Investing in NFTs 199

   Chapter 10 213

   NFT-Based Lending and Staking 213

Chapter 11 .... *236*
The Future of NFTs *236*
CONCLUSION 247

Part I

BLOCKCHAIN - THE NFTs BACKBONE

In this first Part, you are going to be introduced to the world of blockchain. The understanding of how blockchain works is going to enable you to gain a deeper appreciation of how NFTs are created and their possible use-cases.

By understanding how blockchain works, you will be able to follow up on its latest trends and thus be able to explore new opportunities availed by its through NFTs and associated technologies such as Decentralized Finance and be prepared to harness the rewards grab a stake in its future potential.

Important topics covered in this Part include:

- How blockchain works
- Blockchain smart contracts
- Blockchain artwork
- How cryptocurrency works
- How to acquire cryptocurrency
- Stable coins
- How to store your cryptocurrency

Chapter 1

Understanding Blockchain Technology

NFTs are based on blockchain technology. Thus, to be able to understand the nature of NFTs, you must have a basic grasp of what blockchain is, how it works, and its various applications and use-cases.

The technological revolution brought about by blockchain is immense. It has, in just less than a decade, rose from just slightly a million-dollar industry to the current state of almost becoming a multi-trillion-dollar industry. Yes, bitcoin alone is now valued at 1 trillion dollars at a price of roughly $58,000 per bitcoin. Even though this capitalization fluctuates depending on the market price, it is bound to rise.

Yet, bitcoin is just one of the thousands of existing and potential applications of blockchain. Meaning the potential for blockchain is worth trillions of dollars. Already, blockchain is used in managing healthcare registers, research registers, land registers, issuing certificates, banking systems, insurance, supply chain management, logistics management, e-commerce, insurance, among so many other applications.

SO, WHAT IS BLOCKCHAIN?

This is the multi-trillion-dollar question that we are going to address in this chapter briefly. Of course, to exhaustively cover the topic of blockchain would require a whole library of books. Thus, in this book, we will only condense the digestible essentials to enable you to get started. Let's start with the definition...

DEFINITION

A blockchain is a digital logbook of valid transactions taking place within a given network. This digital logbook is a public ledger. It can be accessed and stored by any valid user on the network.

THE NATURE OF BLOCKCHAIN

The rise of cryptocurrencies was facilitated by the advent of blockchain technology. As we have seen in the previous chapter, blockchain is simply a PUBLIC DIGITAL LEDGER.

In accounting, a ledger is used to record every financial transaction. A ledger obeys the DOUBLE-ENTRY principle. In a simplistic perspective, Double Entry is such that an entry (mostly 'debit') in one account is offset by an equivalent counterbalancing (mostly 'credit') exit in another account. Whenever the debit is not equivalent to the credit, then the ledger fails to balance.

A blockchain ledger is like a series of debits and credits – one after another. In a chain of doors, an exit in one door means an entry in another door. As such, a blockchain is a chain of transaction blocks. In this case, a "block" can be considered as an "account." Since, simplistically, an "entry" in one account is offset by an equal "exit" in another account, if the "entry" changes in value, then the "exit" will automatically change to reflect that. If this doesn't happen, then, the irreconcilable state will be evident to the accountants (or "miners") and they will seek to find the cause of this irreconcilable difference between one account (block) with the next account.

However, unlike a standard account or accounting ledger where details are created to be readable and transparent, the details of the blockchain are encrypted. Only the encrypted name of the block is shown.

This is the less technical view of a blockchain. Like in accounting, the debit entry in one account will have details of the corresponding credit entry in another account. This makes it easy for one to know the accounts involved and follow up on the transaction.

How blockchain works

To understand how blockchain works, you have to, first of all, understand what blocks are and how they are linked up together to form a blockchain. In essence, you have to dissect each component that forms it. In addition, you have to understand the blockchain features and protocols that together give the unique characteristics of the blockchain network.

Let's dissect each of these, one at a time:

Block entry

In the blockchain, an entry/exit has three crucial pieces of data:

1. Encrypted information about the previous block
2. Encrypted data recorded in the current block
3. Encrypted details on the current block

Encrypted information about the previous block contains:

1. Identity of the block before it (parent block) – just like the name of the other account in a double entry
2. Encrypted data of the parent block – just like transaction details of an entry/record
3. Encrypted information about it – just like its name (identity)

THE CHAIN LINKS

In a blockchain, the chain link is the information about the identity of the previous block. Every block will have this information. This information will be the same in the current block as in the last block, thus creating a common factor that links them into a chain.

This is the same concept that is applied in relational databases. In a relational database, there is a "foreign key" which is a common key between the two tables that share some common information. This 'foreign key' is equivalent to 'link' in a blockchain. This works the same way as having a common family name as the "surname." The surname or family name links together family members while their first name distinguishes them apart as unique identities.

However, unlike in databases, this key (chain-link) contains all the information about the previous block. That includes the identity of the previous block, the data in it (transaction), and the identity of its parent. This is why a slight change in the data will change the identity code of the block. While, in a database table, even if the rest of the data changes, there will be no change in the "foreign" key.

And this slight change in the block's data will cause a chain reaction to all subsequent and previous blocks.

This makes it impossible to change the data in one block without result in a change in the data in other blocks.

Since the record of each block is stored in a public ledger, everyone has access to it. And no one is restricted from having a whole copy of this ledger. As such, if one makes a change in a block, the rest will know. For this change to be accepted, the rest will have to agree to it and thus update their copies.

This is a strong measure to prevent fraud. On the other hand, since data is encrypted plus the block identity, no one can tell what the block contains except the parties involved. Thus, it is only the parties involved (those who are transacting on the block) that have the private key (encrypted data code). The rest don't know this private key.

BLOCK AND CHAIN

This is the most fundamental characteristic of blockchain. There is blocking and chaining. Blocking means that a block is created which acts as a store (library, container, etc.) of a given set of data and its properties. And chaining is about linking these blocks.

There are three key properties of a block:
- Parent hash - this is the hash (cryptographic information) of the block preceding the previous block. It is just like a biological parent's genetic blueprint (signature) within a

child. Without the parent's genetic blueprint, a child cannot exist.
- Timestamp - this is the time when the block was created. It is just like a biological child's date of birth.
- Block hash - this is the block's unique identity. It is just like a biological child's Birth Certificate. You know that a child's Birth Certificate will not miss having the parent's details such as names, etc. In the case of a block, this simply means that the block hash will contain the parent hash. Thus, block hash = hash (parent hash + block's encrypted data). We can consider the block's data to contain information unique to the block itself (not inherited from the parent)

Like in most stories of Creation, there will be an original block that won't have been 'born' but simply created by 'God'. Like in the Biblical story of creation, this original block is named the 'Genesis' block. Thus, every blockchain will have a genesis block. Genesis block has no parent but simply creator ('God').

The following diagram depicts the essence of a blockchain:

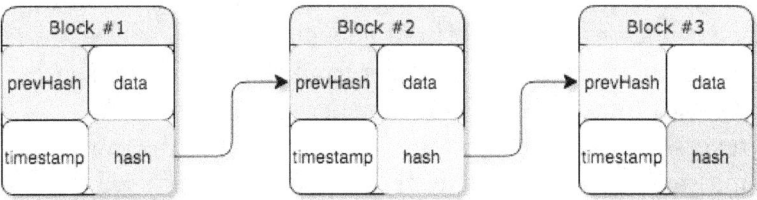

CRYPTOGRAPHY

Cryptography simply refers to generating a secret code as a representation of data/information. Blockchain uses a special form of cryptography known as 'hash'. Hash simply refers to a popular cryptographic standard abbreviated as 'SHA'. For example, Bitcoin uses SHA 256 algorithm. The number '256' simply refers to the number of bits in the final code. We can have 128-bit, 512-bit, 1024 bit, etc. However, SHA 256 and SHA 1024 are the most commonly used.

Blockchain cryptography has the following key properties:

- Hashing - this refers to generating an **immutable code**. That is a code that cannot be decoded. Thus, it cannot be reversed to the raw status it was in before it got encoded. Hashing is used for creating both **public keys** and **private keys**. The public key represents public information about the block, e.g., user name. The private key represents private information about the block, e.g., user password. The private key is used to access encrypted data within a block.
- Chaining - as we have seen before, there is a parent-child relationship in the hashing algorithm. In biological terms, we can look at it as a form of genealogy.
- Encryption - encryption differs from hashing in one sense; it **is not immutable**. Thus, the encrypted code can be reversed to the status prior to encryption, and the raw information read. Thus, encryption is primarily used to represent data in a block. If data were hashed, that simply means it would never be useful as it would never be read.

- Signature - a signature is simply the block's hash. It has all the properties of a block. These include parent signature (parent hash), timestamp, and encrypted data.

HASHING VS. ENCRYPTING

We have talked about the private key as an encrypted data key. However, the public key (information about the identity of the block) is not encrypted. Instead, it is hashed. What is the difference?

Hashing is similar to encrypting. However, you can decode encryption, but you cannot decode a hash. A hash is permanent. A hash can never be reversed.

Since the public key is hashed, it is publicly available, and everyone on the network can see it. But, since no one can reverse or decode it, it sits pretty securely.

Thus, hashing is a sure-proof way of protecting a block and its data. The hash serves as an unbreakable shell, while the private key serves as an entry key to that shell. So, unless this key falls into the wrong hands, no one can enter this shell except you and whoever you authorize it to.

This hashing makes blockchain to be termed as IMMUTABLE. Meaning it cannot be reversed.

Immutability is the essential property of blockchain. And this is achieved through hashing (permanently encoding identity information).

TOKENIZATION

In blockchain terminology, a token is simply a block's signature. What differentiates one token from another is the solution it provides (that is, what is provided within the encryption). For example, a money transfer token could contain instructions such as " I authorize Paul to withdraw $2 from my account". An accounting token could contain instructions such as "Dr. Paul's Cash A/C with $2 and Cr. Mary's Cash A/C with $2" as a way of recording the money transfer instruction.

NETWORKING

For a blockchain to be able to transact, there has to be a network (two or more nodes). For example, in our tokenization example, Mary and Paul are nodes in a network. However, in networking, we will consider the gadgets they are using to transact on the network. For example, Mary's iPad and Paul's PC. Each node has a unique identifier (e.g., IP addressor MAC address) and it is immaterial as to whether Mary is using her iPad to transact or she has authorized her husband to do it on her behalf.

DECENTRALIZATION

This simply means that there is no centralized control. Unlike with most databases, or most accounting ledgers, there is no single central authority in charge of a blockchain. Furthermore, there is no single warehouse for blockchain. Anyone on the network can store a copy of the public ledger. For example, it is not Mary who controls the network. Both Mary and Paul have equal rights to the network, just as all others who are using it.

Decentralization was the overriding consideration that gave birth to the blockchain. The primary goal of blockchain was to overcome the challenges of centralization and the bureaucracy that naturally accompanies it.

Blockchain was designed as a peer-to-peer network. As such, it cut off parasites – yes, those agents in the middle of the chain of distribution who create artificial bottlenecks (roadblocks) so that they can charge toll-free for transactions flowing through their blockages. In the fiat-based financial system, these agents include the Central Banks (centralizing agents), and brokers (banks and other financial intermediaries).

In the fiat-based financial system, the agents take instructions from their bosses – the central banks, leaving the clients (the real money owners) just pawns in the entire parasitic system.

The central bank is abolished through decentralization, and its parasites are not needed and most definitely not wanted. Thus, clients are left to interact with each other, set the rules of engagement, parameters and keep their profits.

In an ideal blockchain system, there is no centralized authority. There is no one patronizing all others on the network, unlike in the traditional network systems.

Democratization

Decisions regarding how to conduct affairs on the network are made through consensus or approval by the majority. For example, for the transaction between Mary and Paul to be recorded in the ledger, there has to be a consensus or approval by the majority on the network.

Anonymity

Since the block's identity is hashed, no one can tell the personal identity of the ownership of a given block.

Consensus

Without a central authority, to make a single entry into the blockchain (that is, to add a block) requires engagement and approval by others, mainly the majority. This consensus makes every transaction public yet anonymous.

PROOFING

Any transaction on the network has to be proofed for its validity before being recorded in the ledger. The process of proofing on a blockchain is called mining. There are specialized mining nodes on the network that do this work before the transaction gets recorded in the ledger. There has to be a consensus among the miners for the proof to be considered successful.

AUTONOMY

Autonomy refers to the ability of each node to work independently on the network without requiring authorization from other nodes. Autonomy is a natural product of decentralization and democratization.

Autonomy also includes the ability to operate anonymously and, to some extent, incognito. Yes, neither Mary nor Paul has to reveal their real-life identities. All that other nodes require is the public key to interact or transact. Thus, neither Paul nor Mary knows each other's real-life identities. That is anonymity.

On the other hand, incognito simply means that other than parties privy to a given transaction, no other party will know their existence on the network except the platform. For example, no one else will know Paul and Mary exists or their public keys except themselves and the platform (including miners).

BLOCKCHAIN NETWORKS

Major blockchain networks based on their unique architecture:

THE BITCOIN NETWORK

Currently, bitcoin is the most valuable currency in the world. As we speak, one bitcoin is equivalent to $58,000. That is more valuable than the worth of those currencies floated by the Petro-funded middle-eastern kingdoms. Yes, Bitcoin is almost overtaking Aramco Oil, the world's largest Petro-dollar company by market capitalization.

How did bitcoin become such a precious currency? The best way to appreciate this journey is to walk down bitcoin's memory late – get an understanding of its origin and its history.

HOW DID BITCOIN COME ABOUT?

Bitcoin's origin is attributed to Satoshi Nakamoto - a nondescript character deemed to have created Bitcoin and first published it in 2009. However, the concept of crypto-currency was first mooted by Wei Dei in 1998.

What is Bitcoin?

Bitcoin is a consensus and decentralized network that allows completely digital money (cryptocurrency) to be exchanged.

The following are essential features of Bitcoin:

1. It is a system – Bitcoin is a system where bitcoins are used. In this case, a bitcoin is the actual currency, just like a dollar, a pound, a shilling, etc. However, sometimes the terms are used interchangeably so you can differentiate by understanding the context within which they are used.
2. It is a network – Bitcoin is a network that allows many users to interact in creating and exchanging bitcoins.
3. It is digital – there is no physical currency or physical entity. The entire currency (bitcoin) and commodity (Bitcoin) are electronic.
4. It is cryptic – bitcoins are cryptic (secret codes); thus it is represented by secret codes. That's why it is called cryptocurrency (a cryptic currency). Weirdly, even the Bitcoin founder (Satoshi Nakamoto) is cryptic.
5. It is decentralized – Bitcoin is decentralized such that the creation of bitcoins is not controlled by any central authority and is neither attributed to any central authority such as a central bank or a specific government.
6. It is peer-to-peer – Bitcoin system is a peer-to-peer system such that its value and exchange are determined by consenting parties.
7. It is anonymous – users can hold multiple bitcoins without having them attached to any personal details.
8. It is fast- it takes a maximum of 10 minutes for a Bitcoin transaction to complete
9. It has the lowest transaction fee – unlike other modes of online transactions that charge between 2% to 5%, the Bitcoin transaction fee is extremely minimal.
10. It is irreversible – once a person transfers bitcoin to you, they cannot repudiate the transfer. This helps to save

transferees from the unexpected mischievousness of an unscrupulous transferor.

Exploring Bitcoin Mining

So, precisely what is Bitcoin mining?

Technically, Bitcoin mining is the process that involves using computer technology and resources to process transactions, secure the integrity of the network, and keeping everyone in the system synchronized.

How does Bitcoin mining work?

When processing transactions in Bitcoin, the bitcoins have to be created. The bitcoins are created by using a particular set of software and computer hardware to solve complex mathematical problems using complex algorithms and once the results are proven to be correct, you are rewarded with encryption which is registered on the network as a cryptocurrency (called bitcoin).

The algorithm is complex such that every new bitcoin released becomes part of the new complex algorithm for solving mathematical problems. This means that to solve a problem, you must put all bitcoins ever released as part of the algorithm. It is such a daunting task that those who are only interested in the business part of Bitcoin would rather leave its mining to crypto mining experts.

Proof-of-Work and Mining

We've already discussed proofing as one of the blockchain functionality. Proof-of-work is just one of the proofing mechanisms.

We have also indicated that the process of proofing on a blockchain is called mining. Bitcoin, being a blockchain platform, employs both proofing and mining methodology.

Where do you mine bitcoins?
You use your computer hardware (which at the moment must be so powerful considering the millions of bitcoins so far mined) plus a set of sophisticated software to mine bitcoins while at the same time interacting with the bitcoin network (since every bitcoin ever released must be part and parcel of the complex algorithm to be followed in solving a complex mathematical problem). Therefore, the bitcoins are mined from the network and your computer and software only serve as tools to mine them.

How much can you mine?
You can mine as much as you can. However, the upper limit of what can ever be mined is set as 21 million bitcoins. Therefore, hypothetically, the maximum you can mine is equivalent to 21 million minus all the bitcoins that have been mined so far.

THE ETHEREUM NETWORK

Ethereum is the second most popular cryptocurrency. It also ranks among the most trusted and valued cryptocurrencies. Thus, if you feel that, for specific reasons, you cannot buy bitcoins then, Ethereum (Ether) is the next best option. Ether is the coin (currency), while Ethereum is the platform. It is common for people to use the term 'Ethereum' when they are actually referring to 'Ether.' You can distinguish the two based on the context in which they are applied.

What is Ethereum?

Ethereum was invented by Vitalik Buterin. What makes Ethereum so popular is its flexibility. The ability of programmers to create their blockchain is what distinguished Ethereum from Bitcoin. It is this feature that propelled the creation of decentralized Apps (dApps). Initial Coin Offering (ICO) became another possible feature due to this programmability. ICOs became a popular funding vehicle for programmers to fund their dApp projects.

In turn, ICOs increased Ethereum's capitalization. It has enabled many entrepreneurs to raise funds for their own Ethereum projects. Programmable blockchain and custom Ethereum apps have made Ethereum more appealing to financial institutions than Bitcoin.

Another popular feature of Ethereum is the so-called 'Smart Contracts' (self-executing conditional payments). This is because, unlike Bitcoin, Ethereum blockchain not only validates a set of accounts and balances but also 'States'. States are complex contracts and programs. DAO is Ethereum's smart contract. The downside of this flexibility is that it creates an enabling environment for hackers. However, Ethereum has been able to come up with sophisticated security features since the initial hacking of its original DAO. It came up with more secure variants of DAO, such as DigixDAO and Augur.

To ward off hackers, Ethereum has come up with 'Proof of Stake' (PoS) as a form of the transaction verification system. This is much more efficient than the traditional 'Proof of Work' (PoW) that Bitcoin and some other cryptocurrencies use.

As of now, Ethereum is more of a family of cryptocurrencies rather than one cryptocurrency.

ETHEREUM 2.0 VS ETH (PROOF-OF-STAKE VS PROOF-OF-WORK)

The biggest difference between Ethereum 2.0 and Ethereum 1.0 (ETH) rests in the process of achieving consensus. While Ethereum 2.0 employs Proof-of-Stake (PoS), Ethereum 1.0 employs Proof-of-Work (PoW)

Under the proof-of-work, all miners are treated equally; as such, there has to be a common consensus among all participating miners for a transaction to be validated. However, under proof-of-stake, not all miners are treated equally. Miners that hold bigger stakes in terms of the amount of mining under their belt are given a higher say in establishing the transaction validity.

ADVANTAGES OF ETHEREUM 2.0 OVER ETHEREUM 1.0

Apart from this difference in consensus mechanism, there are lots of improvement that comes with Ethereum 2.0

The following are some of the improvements/advantages:

- **Sharding** – sharding means that the Ethereum ledger is distributed. As such, a node needs not to have the entire ledger but a part of it that is relevant to its needs. Therefore, different nodes can have different parts of the ledger, and if one needs to use a certain part of this ledger, the person will be directed to that node or set of nodes that have it. Sieving through a massive ledger just to get one transaction has been one of the leading causes of slow speed on the blockchain network (Bitcoin and Ethereum included). Sharding speeds up access to a transaction record within the ledger.
- **Parallelization (multithreading)** – the old Ethereum was based on complete serialization. As such, a transaction had to be performed one after the other in sequence. It was not possible to perform multiple transactions at the same time. However, with Ethereum 2.0, hundreds of parallel transaction processing can take place at the same time. Thanks to sharding and other techniques.
- **High scalability** – due to sharding and proof-of-stake, Ethereum 2.0 has become highly scalable and thus can hold up to 10,000 tps (transactions per second) compared to the less scalable Ethereum that could only hold up to 30 tps.
- **Energy efficiency** – The PoW mechanism under Ethereum 1.0 was extremely energy-intensive. Thus, there was a lot of energy wastage in the mining process. The PoS mechanism under Ethereum 2.0 is comparatively more energy-efficient
- **Speed** – as we have seen, Ethereum 2.0 can process up to 10,000 tps (transactions per second) compared to Ethereum 1.0 that could only process up to 30 tps. This translates to a speed that is over 300 times faster.

Disadvantages of Ethereum 2.0

- **Security** – while PoW can be equated with "Prisoner-of-Work" due to the sheer energy expended in doing work, PoS can be equated with "Prisoner-of-Stakes" due to its dependency on a few stakeholders with big stakes. In the PoS, there is a possibility of big stakeholders conspiring to act in a manner that may be selfish and injuries to other stakeholders on the network. While Ethereum 2.0 has endeavored to overcome this likelihood of conspiracy by requiring at least 16,384 validators on the network to proof a transaction. It has also engaged the service of independent validators (auditors) to counter the likelihood of a malfeasant conspiracy on the network.
- **Risk of Cliquism** – under Ethereum 2.0, direct democracy (where all nodes had equal rights to participate in the decision-making process) has been replaced with representative democracy (where big stakeholders got special rights to decide). This raises the potential for a clique of big stakeholders manipulating the system for their selfish gains – just as big politicians conspire to exploit the masses in a representative democracy.

The Lisk Network

We cannot talk of Bitcoin and Ethereum without mentioning Lisk. Lisk is one of the unique blockchain networks that are closer to Ethereum than Bitcoin in terms of features. Yet, it is strikingly different from Ethereum.

What is Lisk?

Lisk is a blockchain platform that was established in 2016 to enable easier and faster development and deployment of DApps. It boasts of efficient proofing, rapid deployment of DApps, and less congestion on its blockchain.

KEY FEATURES

The following key features make Lisk a unique kind of blockchain network:

    1) Lisk Core

This is the main software that runs the Lisk network. It is like Operating Software (OS) for PCs.

Lisk Core is responsible for enforcing protocols, synchronizing the operations of various computers on the network, and ensuring optimized and smooth operations on the network.

    2) Lisk SDK

Lisk's Software Development Kit (SDK) is an assortment of various tools used for creating DApps on the Lisk network. Some people replace the term 'Software' with 'Sidechain' as it is primarily about building sidechains and DApps to run on them.

The following features describe the Lisk SDK:

Development language

Lisk SDK is developed using native Javascript. As such, application developers need to use Javascript to create their DApps.

The choice of Javascript is strategic:

- **To significantly cut down on the learning curve** –most, if not all, software developers know Javascript. Thus, unlike other DApps development platforms, developers need not learn a new programming language. For example, if you have to create DApps on Ethereum, you will need to learn Solidity or Serpent. Thus, the time that would have otherwise been spent on learning a new language is spent on creating a new DApp.
- **To attract more DApp developers** – Since Javascript is one of the world's most widely known programming languages, many developers won't be discouraged from trying out Lisk.
- **To promote wide adoption** – Javascript is a language that can run virtually on all machines. This means that, whether you are using Windows, Linux, macOS, or any other OS, you are still at home with Lisk.
- **To increase openness and transparency** – since most programmers have at least a basic knowledge of Javascript, it is easy for them to read and audit Lisk DApps. This helps to reduce the risk of malicious programs disguised as DApps.

Components

Components are simply tools that enable the development of Sidechains and DApps. Lisk SDK has three main components:

- Lisk framework: Lisk framework is the one responsible for facilitating the interaction between the various modules of DApp.
- Lisk elements: This comprises the various coding libraries that are used to create DApps.
- Lisk Commander: This is a tool that lets users interact with the network.

3) Sidechains

A sidechain is simply a separate blockchain operating within the Lisk network. Thus, a developer creates a sidechain and then builds a DApp on it.

The sidechains are bound to the main chain at the time of creation. Unlike the main chain, sidechains are customizable and thus can meet the specific needs of the developer.

Furthermore, sidechains help to avoid overloading the main chain during the DApp development phase.

4) LSK coin

To maintain the Lisk network, some fee has to be charged. LSK coin is the means by which this fee is paid.

5) Delegated Proof-of-Stake (dPoS)

DPoS is a consensus mechanism that allows users to vote on the computer that will build the next block on the Lisk network.

However, the users don't vote directly. Instead, they vote for their representatives through a delegated system. As such, the users vote for 101 delegates. Each delegate can then create a block. There are 101 blocks per cycle. Each block cycle takes about 16 minutes, with every block taking about 16 seconds to create.

LSK coin is used as the vote. A coin used in the voting is deemed to have been 'staked.' Thus, a voter has to have a stake in the voting process. In this regard, a stake is simply the 'right to vote or its proof thereof.'

DIFFERENCE BETWEEN LISK AND ETHEREUM

Both Lisk and Ethereum are platforms for developing DApps. However, they employ different approaches to this development process.

The following are the distinguishing features between Lisk and Ethereum:

- **Programming language (JavaScript vs solidity)** - Lisk uses pure javascript (preferably ES6). It also allows the use of Typescript. On the other hand, Ethereum uses Solidity. Even though Solidity is based on Javascript, it is an extremely customized language that requires considerable learning. The advantage of using pure JavaScript (for JavaScript programmers) is that time is spent on learning how to apply JavaScript to building DApps rather than learning how to program. It is rare to find an experienced and professional programmer who doesn't have a fair knowledge of JavaScript.
- **Proofing (Voting vs mining)** - Lisk employs a voting mechanism to proof a given transaction. On the other hand, Ethereum uses a mining process to proof a given blockchain transaction. Mining is not only time-consuming but also resource-intensive. This makes it slower, laborious, and more expensive compared to Lisk.

- **Consensus mechanism (dPoS vs PoW/S)** - While Ethereum is gradually shifting away from Proof-of-Work (PoW) in Ethereum 1.0 to Proof-of-Stake (PoS) in Ethereum 2.0, most of the transactions still rely heavily on the PoW mechanism (Ethereum 1.0). Lisk, from inception, started with PoS. However, to make PoS faster, cheaper, more secure, and less laborious, only delegates are involved in the PoS. This limits the number of Stakeholders to just 101 delegates as opposed to Ethereum that would allow anyone with a stake to participate in direct proofing. Thus, even if Ethereum completely switches to PoS, it will still be more resource-intensive, more expensive, and likely slower than Lisk. Well, Ethereum can make itself faster than Lisk by applying more sophisticated technology – but that means more redesigning effort, more resources, and more computing power.
- **Execution environment (Sidechain vs Mainchain)** - Both Lisk and Ethereum have Virtual Machines. However, unlike Ethereum that relies heavily on the main chain to build and run DApps, Lisk has Sidechains where DApps are built and run. The Sidechains are then linked with the main chain. This serves to free up the main chain from queuing, jam and clogging. Thus, the main chain is utilized more efficiently and cost-effectively.
- **Executors (master nodes vs miner nodes)** - While Ethereum relies on miner nodes for proofing, Lisk relies on master nodes. Each delegate is a master node. Thus, there are 101 master nodes required to effect a Lisk block.
- **DApp costing (Developers vs Miners)** - On Lisk, it is DApp developers that determine the cost of a given DApp. On Ethereum, it is Miners who establish the cost of a DApp. As such, Lisk rewards developers and thus incentivizes them to create more DApps.

BLOCKCHAIN AND CYBERSECURITY

With our increasing reliance on cyber networks, cybersecurity has become a core concern that will continue to grow as networks evolve. Blockchain is a cyber network system that has attracted increasing attention and, therefore, concerns around security risks.

Fintech has been the most prominent application of blockchain. Cybersecurity breaches have led to <u>losses of billions of dollars worth of cryptocurrency</u>, raising alarm bells, starting a debate as to whether blockchain is an asset or liability in cybersecurity.

It is crucial to compare blockchain vulnerabilities/benefits with non-blockchain vulnerabilities/benefits to having an opinion in this debate. This comparison makes it easier to establish whether blockchain is indeed an asset or a liability to cybersecurity.

NON-BLOCKCHAIN VULNERABILITIES

- DDoS attacks - Security experts estimates that a large enterprise loses between <u>*$2.5 million and 6.5 million*</u> per DDoS attack.
- Malware planting - NotPetya malware alone is estimated to have cost the world <u>*$10 billion*</u> in damages, with Maersk being its most prominent victim that lost almost $300 million in lost revenue.
- Credential stuffing is common with online access systems where hackers phish for passwords that they then use to infiltrate the system. They can also use this method to learn how systems generate passwords and replicate them for brute-force attacks.

- Ransomware attacks - Ransomware alone costs the world about *$5 billion* and is estimated to rise to *$11.5 billion* in 2019. Wannacry alone cost the world about $4 billion in loss
- Man-in-the-middle attacks - In Europe, these attacks were used to steal *6 million Euros*.
- Attacks on transactions (process) - these are attacks that aim to seize a given critical process and then influence it to achieve the attacker's objectives.

How blockchain safeguards against non-blockchain vulnerabilities

Due to the decentralized, distributed, and often cloud-based nature of the blockchain network, DDoS attacks and malware planting are much more challenging to implement, and it is nearly impossible to cripple systems with these.

The robust cryptography used by the blockchain network makes it difficult for credential stuffing, ransomware attacks, man-in-the-middle attacks, and attacks on transactions (process) to be successful. Furthermore, the proof-of-work and consensus validation mechanisms of blockchain networks add an extra layer of cybersecurity.

Characteristic features of the blockchain network which help ward

OFF COMMON NON-BLOCKCHAIN SYSTEM ATTACKS

The following are unique features of blockchain that boost its security:

- Consensus validation mechanism
- Hashing and encryption
- Distributed architecture
- Transparency through consensus validation mechanism
- Cloud storage

BLOCKCHAIN'S UNIQUE VULNERABILITIES

- Post-attack recovery failures - while immutability helps guard against the most common risks on non-blockchain systems, have unique disadvantages. When attacks successfully happen, recovery is not possible.
- Credential security risks - due to the distributed nature accompanied by democratization, anonymity, and autonomy of the multiple entities on the network, it becomes difficult to manage identities, control access rights, clearly demarcate roles, guard private key storage, enhance security configurations and respond quickly enough to compromises. Within the first half of 2018 alone, blockchain cryptocurrencies have lost over $1 billion due to this risk. However, these risks can be extensively mitigated by permission blockchain frameworks such as Hyperledger Fabric and Corda.

CAN BLOCKCHAIN VULNERABILITIES BE CURED BY NON-BLOCKCHAIN SOLUTIONS?

Unfortunately, post-attack recovery failure remains the main outstanding vulnerability. However, this is a sacrifice one has to pay for the nature of blockchain (immutability) to work, especially in permissionless blockchain systems such as Bitcoin and Ethereum. Permissioned blockchain systems such as Fabric and Corda have shown that such challenges attributed to permissionless systems can be solved while enjoying the benefits of blockchain.

WHAT CAN BE CONCLUDED ON BLOCKCHAIN AND CYBERSECURITY

Blockchain is still a new technology with greater room for improvement. While there are several systemic risks inherent in blockchain technology, they are far less compared to non-blockchain systems with similar attributes (e.g., based on public/private distributed protocol).

On a cost-benefit scale, the security benefits of the blockchain system outweigh the security risks by far. On the other hand, the blockchain system has fewer vulnerabilities compared to non-blockchain systems with similar protocols - distributed, public and decentralized. This simply means that, overall, blockchain is a net asset.

On a comparative scale, blockchain remains a net asset to cybersecurity – a net asset whose value is likely going to increase as the technology matures.

Chapter 2

Blockchain Applications and Use-Cases

NFT is one of the many applications of blockchain. NFT also relies on other applications such as smart contracts, cryptocurrency (for funding), and trading platforms, among others, to fully function.

In this chapter, we are going to explore various blockchain applications, some of which are already being utilized by NFT while the bulk of them have a future NFT utility potential.

BLOCKCHAIN DAPPS

DApp is a short form of 'Decentralized Application.' Specifically, DApps are blockchain applications since, by nature, blockchain is decentralized.

The difference between DApp and other apps is that DApps reside on the blockchain network, and as such, they have no one central location where they can be found. They are distributed.

The significance of this decentralization and distribution is that there is no point in failure. For example, if a hacker successfully brings one node down, the DApp will still run on dozens, hundreds, or thousands of other nodes – depending on how many nodes are on a given blockchain network.

This provides a fail-safe mechanism against hacking and node failure.

How to create your own DApp

You can create your own DApp!

While it is necessary to have blockchain programming knowledge to create a DApp, it is not a must. You can let someone else do the programming part. Indeed, there are many programmers ready to develop a DApp for you at an affordable price. Leave that work to them.

It is essential to have the entrepreneurial know-how of what it entails to successfully initiate and complete a DApp project.

The steps involved are:

    1) Learn and understand the blockchain concept

The first and most fundamental step is to have an assured understanding of the whole concept of blockchain. This step is extremely important as it will enable you to sail through steps (2) to (5), especially when designing the right architecture.

We have already considered briefly what Blockchain is. In furtherance of this, let's look at some of the critical concepts behind blockchain:

- Block and Chain
- Cryptography (hashing)
- Tokenization
- Networking
- Decentralization
- Democratization
- Proofing
- Autonomy

2) Set your goals

Goal setting is crucial as it will guide you through the rest of the steps. What are your goals in build your blockchain Dapp? This question should be the primary question that you must address.

Obviously, each Dapp project has its own unique goals; otherwise, you would not need to waste time repeating what others have already done.

While there is no need to repeat here what is abundantly covered in business and management books about goal setting, let's just remind ourselves that we need to set SMART goals.

SMART simply means that a goal must be:

- Specific
- Measurable
- Achievable

- Relevant
- Timely

Grab a good business management book to learn more about SMART goals. Nonetheless, I would advise you to go further than SMART to set the SMARTEST goal that stands out from the crowd. In addition to being SMART, the goal must also be:

- Empowering
- Stimulating
- Transformational

Of course, blockchain is a disruptive technology. Thus, it must disrupt the SMART concept by being the SMARTEST of them all. A blockchain Dapp solution must empower the user more than any other solution available. It must stimulate the user to 'want it now!' and 'more!' Lastly, it must transform the user's current status to a new paradigm.

Don't forget! You are building a business case for your Dapp. It is this business case that you will eventually package as a whitepaper. Furthermore, see the SMARTness through the user's lens, not your own.

3) Establish the required use-case

Squeeze the pain! Take yourself as a doctor who is trying to establish the pain point on a patient. How painful is it? Is it such excruciating? The more painful it is, the more powerful is the justification for a potent painkiller solution. Why else would you want to create a powerful painkiller if the pain is so light such that over-the-counter paracetamol can do away with it?

In simple terms, don't waste your effort in trying to find a blockchain solution in a situation where blockchain won't make much of a difference to the already existing non-blockchain solution. Yes, if your blockchain Dapp can't Empower, Stimulate, and Transform, then dump it!

What is the user's pain point that my Dapp will heal? That should be your rallying question. It is the question that you must address. And by addressing this question, you will have deciphered the use case.

4) Establish an appropriate consensus mechanism

Blockchain resides within a democratic state. If you desire to have a centralized command, try a 'communist' state. Then, you have to give it to the people "nodes." As a creator, what you need is to establish the 'genesis' constitution that will guide the affairs of this newly formed democratic state. Afterward, it is up to the 'people' to set rules regarding how to run their common affairs. They, too, can change the constitution, provided that they do not dissolve the state.

Well, politics aside, what this simply means is that there has to be a way by which the nodes achieve consensus. Do not forget that, even in real life, no value can be created without an agreement.

In the blockchain, the following are the commonly used methods of achieving consensus:

- Proof of Work
- Proof of Stake
- Proof of Elapsed Time
- Proof of Provenance

Other methods include:

- Byzantine fault-tolerant (BFT)
- Simplified BFT
- Redundant BFT
- Derived PBFT (Proof of BFT)
- Federated Byzantine Agreement
- Federated consensus
- Round Robin
- Delegated Proof of Stake
- Deposit based consensus

The mechanism to use depends on the blockchain platform (network) upon which you intend to establish the DApp.

5) Establish the right architecture

A DApp architecture is elaborated through a blueprint. This blueprint explains how the DApp will be constructed, where it will be hosted, what it will do, and how it will work.

The following are some of the core elements of a DApp blueprint:

- A definition of platform parameters
- The construction methodology – this includes the coding language, team collaboration, and the collaboration mechanism e.g. agile, scrum, Jira, etc.
- The method and procedures of interaction between various nodes in the transaction process
- The proofing and consensus mechanism and how both are going to be attained

6) Create a Whitepaper

In simple terms, a Whitepaper is a business plan of your Dapp project. It incorporates technical, financial, and publicity aspects of your project.

All the previous steps we have discussed get distilled into a Whitepaper. The structure and content of your Whitepaper will depend on intent, purpose, and target audience.

For example, if the overriding intent of your Whitepaper is to attract funding for your project, then, it will be designed to attract the ears and win the hearts of investors. On the other hand, if the overriding intent of your Whitepaper is to attract developers, then it will be more technically detailed in terms of engineering. In case your Whitepaper is aimed at gaining wider publicity, then, it will heavily focus on squeezing the pain points in order to justify the project.

Whichever your intent or purpose, it is extremely important to create a Whitepaper prior to embarking on the development phase. The Whitepaper helps to consolidate all your previous steps. Ultimately, the Whitepaper provides a soul for your project. It is this soul that will guide you in coming up with a matching body in the development phase.

7) Inject resources into the project

Just as a car feeds on fuel, projects feed on resources. Your DApp project needs to be adequately resourced.

The core resources that your DApp needs are:

- Skills
- Organization
- Capital

The skills needed depends on the nature and scope of your DApp project. However, at a bare minimum, the following skills are required:

- Backend software development skills
- Front-end software development skills
- Software testing and auditing skills
- Support skills

Organization refers to how resources and skills are laid out to interact in order to actualize the DApp project. Organization includes:

- Managing skills
- Managing resources
- Managing processes

Capital refers to resources used in generating further resources. Capital is classified into two broad categories:

Fiscal capital – this refers to the infrastructure laid out to attract or generate financial resources. It includes financial tools, financial processes, financial resources, and financial management.

Physical capital – this refers to the non-fiscal infrastructure. In the DApp project, physical capital includes the blockchain network platform, IDE (integrated development environment), among others.

8) Code and test the DApp

Now that you have the blueprint (skeleton) and the whitepaper (soul), the next step is to create the DApp (mind) so that it can coordinate the blockchain (body) functions to execute your set goals.

The good thing is that you do not have to be a software engineer or programmer to code the DApp. All you need is to be an entrepreneur. There are many DApp programmers that you can hire on a freelance basis to do the coding on your behalf while you focus on other functions such as funding, marketing, and management.

9) Launch the DApp

Once you have the DApp complete, you can then launch it. That is, make it available on the blockchain network to run and execute the functions. DApp is a product. Make sure that the launch is accompanied by technical documentation, user documentation, support contacts, and support tools.

10) Market the Dapp

Don't let your DApp sit idle on the blockchain network, create awareness about its availability and use-cases (need-satisfying functions). Explain to potential users the gainful benefits of using your DApp.

Again, like coding, you don't have to sweat about marketing. There are many freelance marketers that you can hire to do this for you.

BLOCKCHAIN BUSINESS

Blockchain has many business applications and use-cases. There is just a lot that has not been explored or exploited as far as blockchain business is concerned.

Nonetheless, the most fundamental applications of blockchain in business are in three main domains:

- Exchange of value
- Storage of value
- Smart business contracts

EXCHANGE OF VALUE

Business is about the exchange of value. For example, a seller receives value (price) in exchange for parting with a given product/service. On the other hand, the buyer receives value (product) in exchange for sacrifice (price).

Traditionally, money has been used as a medium of exchange of value. With blockchain, cryptocurrency has taken over this role of being a medium of exchange of value.

CRYPTOCURRENCY

Cryptocurrency is a blockchain-based digital currency. It is used as a medium of exchange of value just the way conventional (fiat) currencies such as the dollar, euro, sterling pound, etc., are used.

To learn more about cryptocurrency, please read Chapter 3.

CROSS-BORDER REMITTANCES

Fiat currencies have been used for ages as a medium of exchange across borders. However, given the volatility of these fiat currencies due to changes in the economic situation of each country, thus affecting its national currency, it has been a tough job to make cross-border remittances.

Cryptocurrencies, though volatile, avoid the complicated remittance mechanism through the extremely expensive international bureaucracies such as SWIFT, PayPal, Skrill, among others.

Since cryptocurrencies are borderless and thus do not need to be converted to national currencies, they are not only cheap but also extremely fast. Take an example of Stellar Lumens; they are extremely affordable cryptocurrencies that can easily be used from micro-payments that could be as small as a millionth of a dollar.

STORAGE OF VALUE

Just as money is used as a measure of stored value, cryptocurrency can also be used for the same purpose. Though, unlike gold, cryptocurrency is highly volatile. Due to this volatility, cryptocurrency can easily inflate and erode the stored value of the property thus distorting its true worth.

SMART BUSINESS CONTRACTS

Business is about contracts. Every business transaction is a contract, whether written or not, explicit or not. Without digging into the legal technicalities, three salient features of a contract are:

- Offer: one party (e.g., the buyer) makes an offer to buy a certain product.
- Acceptance: the other party (e.g., the seller) accepts the offer made by the buyer.
- Consideration: this is the exchangeable value of sacrifice. It is often expressed in terms of price. For example, price is a measure of equivalent sacrifice by both the buyer and the seller in the exchange of value. The buyer sacrifices value (e.g., a part of wage) whose worth is equivalent to the price and the seller sacrifices the product (e.g., cost plus profit margin) whose value is equivalent to the price offered.

A smart business contract automates the matching of offer and acceptance and the ensuing exchange of value based on the already algorithmically established protocols.

BLOCKCHAIN SMART PROPERTY

Smart property is a type of property that is either fully blockchain-based or whose functionality is blockchain-enabled.

SMART KEYS

Smart keys are those blockchain cryptographic keys that allow only authorized access to a given property. For example, a smart car key can be operated using a PIN linked to the blockchain.

When you lose such a key, there is no risking through uncontrolled physical duplication. The blockchain network automatically replicates the key.

Apart from cars, smart keys can be used in remote property hire and leasing services such as Airbnb, self-driven cars, space rentals (such as box rentals, parking space rental, etc.), among others. The convenience of automatic replication of the keys (if lost), easy changing of PIN, and remote accessibility make it the most ideal as no physical presence of the key/property owner is required.

SMART GADGETS (THINGS)

Smart gadgets are those gadgets that can be used to execute specific functions based on algorithmic protocols.

Examples include dongles, hard wallets, wearables, SIM cards, QR Cards, etc.

SMART EMBEDS

Smart embeds are those gadgets that have embedded software and sensors such that they can work autonomously or through remote control.

Examples include RFID embeds, etc.

BLOCKCHAIN SMART CONTRACTS

Contracts are essential in all forms of transactions, be they business or otherwise. For so long as there is an exchange of value, or the intention to do so, a contract exists. Blockchain makes contracts easier through smart contracts.

WHAT ARE SMART CONTRACTS?

Smart contracts are self-executing digital codes that contain algorithmic parameters about predefined conditions which parties to the agreement must meet before it is executed.

Smart contracts are self-executing in the sense that there is an automated algorithmic confirmation of met conditions without human intervention. As such, neither party to the agreement or an external party can manipulate this confirmation.

For example, in a land-buying deal, both the buyer and the seller can create a smart contract based on a digital title deed. Once the buyer pays for the agreed price of the land, the algorithm within the smart contract automatically changes the ownership details on the digital title deed such that details of the seller are replaced with the details of the buyer. There is no going to the attorney's office for such a transfer to happen.

Ethereum Smart Contracts

Smart contracts have gained lots of traction as a form of entering into binding contracts. This is primarily due to their fast, efficient, and cost-economic self-executing nature.

We cannot mention blockchain smart contracts without mentioning Ethereum Smart Contracts. Right from inception, the Ethereum network was created with Smart Contracts in mind.

Currently, the Ethereum network enjoys a near-monopoly as far as hosting smart contracts is concerned. It is the industry standard upon which other smart contract networks are based. Thus, understanding Ethereum smart contracts make it easier to understand other networks' smart contracts.

What features make smart contracts unique?

Smart contracts have become popular due to the following unique features:

    1) Autonomous

Once algorithmic parameters are set, there is no need for human involvement or risk of human interference. The heavy work rests in ensuring that the algorithm is correct and accurate. Once that is done, everything else is left to the self-executing mechanism.

This autonomy guarantees non-interference, especially by an untrustworthy party or a devious third party.

2) Secured

Due to the nature of cryptography that involves both encryption and hashing and the blockchain's proofing mechanism, smart contracts are incredibly secure. There is no other analog or digital contract that is more secure than smart contracts.

3) Interruption Free

As we have already seen, the algorithmic nature of the smart contract means that no person can interrupt the self-executing mechanism.

4) Trustless

While traditional transactions require mutual trust and utmost good faith as a prerequisite to concluding a contract, smart contracts do not require that. For so long as both parties agree to the preset conditions, no party needs to trust the other as far as execution is concerned. This is because neither party can interfere with or stop the execution. This is unlike the traditional contract whereby one party to the agreement can fail or refuse to execute his/her part of the deal.

Furthermore, due to the decentralized nature of the network and the anonymous cryptographic nature of the details, no third party can deliberately interfere with this execution. In the traditional system, an overriding authority such as the government or its agents can thwart a contract's execution to the disadvantage of the involved parties. Governments cannot interfere with smart contracts.

5) Cost-effective

If you have ever gone to a lawyer to prepare a transaction of value, you would realize how expensive it is. Furthermore, there is a minimum fee below which a lawyer cannot accept to draft the contract on behalf of the parties. This means that contracts of small values such as $100 or less will not be cost-effective.

When it comes to smart contracts, you do not need a lawyer. Furthermore, you can make smart contracts at any convenient time. The same is not the case with the attorney's office. You cannot walk into the attorney's office in the wee hour of the night to draft or execute a contract, but you can do this with a smart contract. The office is on your computer and within reach of your fingertips. Time is costly. Smart contracts can save tons of it.

6) Fast Performance

With an exception to some delays in the network, the execution of smart contracts is almost instant. All that is needed is algorithmic confirmation that all set parameters have been met.

7) Accurate and Error-Free

For so long as smart contracts have been properly programmed, no errors will take place during the execution, unlike the so many errors that often take place during the execution of traditional contracts. The execution is accurate and error-free.

WHAT ARE SOME OF THE COMMON USE-CASES OF SMART CONTRACTS?

Smart contract use-cases are rapidly expanding as more people get acquainted with how they work. The use-cases are many, varied, and diverse.

To mention but just a few, the following are the most popular use-cases:

1) Digital Identity

Digital identity is one of the most important assets in the digital world. Thus, it needs full protection. Identity theft is extremely common on the internet today. This is because once a person steals your identity, the person can forge documents, steal your bank funds using forged credit card details, or even blackmail you for a ransom.

With traditional banking, you entrust lots of details with banks and other financial institutions for the sake of complying with KYC (Know-Your-Customer) requirements as set out by the government through its agencies. The KYC details are stored in the traditional databases. Cases of hackers gaining access to these digital databases and thus stealing KYC information are rampant.

Smart contracts help to stop this theft of digital identity. Smart contracts rely on KYH (Know-Your-Hash) instead of KYC. KYH ensures your anonymity such that no one knows your identity except you.

Thus, KYH is a self-sovereign identity (SSI). You are a sovereign entity on the decentralized network. As such, no one except you knows your personal identity.

The history of your engagement in Smart contracts can uplift your profile such that decentralized financial institutions can easily lend to you without having to conduct laborious background checks. They do not need traditional referees. And the good thing with smart contracts is that there is no room for you to be tempted to spoil your reputation.

2) High Securities

Due to the immutable nature of some critical parts of the smart contract, cryptography, anonymity, and the self-executing mechanism, smart contracts are extremely secure. The lack of intermediaries reduces the risk further as there is no data entrusted in the hands of persons that the parties to the transaction have no control over.

This reduces operational risks, which are incredibly high in the banking, insurance, and even the security sector itself.

3) Cross-Border Payments

When it comes to cross-border trade, financing transactions become extremely complex due to the huge array of third parties involved.

Furthermore, due to the complexity and differences in legal jurisdiction between the cross-border parties, it becomes even harder to secure trade financing as the mechanism to hold the deviant party accountable is highly complex.

Smart contracts can simply trade finance, transfer of cross-border property deeds, letters of credit, freight insurance, and many other cross-border transactions and processes.

With smart contracts, relying on the intervention of a foreign government that may be unwilling to hold the deviant party who happens to be its citizen is largely eliminated.

The use of smart contract escrows can help mitigate the risk of one party delivering merchandise and ending up without being paid or the other party paying while the merchandise fails to be delivered.

4) Loans and Mortgages

Loans and mortgages are often complicated by the process of custodianship of the title to the property being mortgaged, the title transfer process, and compliance with the payment schedule.

The use of the digital title in smart contracts effectively handles the custodianship issue. There is no need for a third party to keep the title safe or act as a witness. Furthermore, there are no nagging delays that often accompany the laborious transfer of ownership in the traditional system.

However, since loans and mortgages are subject to property laws of a given jurisdiction, it means the government entities responsible need to have a system that is adaptive to smart contracts.

5) Financial Data Recording

The traditional ledger system requires a bookkeeper to manually enter financial data (whether in the paper book or an accounting app).

With smart contracts, this entry is done automatically. As such, there is no need to have a bookkeeper as one needs to check the historical logs.

What more? It is the cheapest form of financial recording. The cost of financial fraud, common in traditional financial systems, is almost non-existent as smart contract transactions are very transparent.

6) Government

Governments are almost synonymous with bottle-neck bureaucracy. This bureaucracy hurts more than it benefits. The long chain of government transactions often arises out of the need to verify transactions such that the more officials involved in the transaction, the lesser the risk of collusion.

Smart contracts not only eliminate this risk of collusion but also makes this long chain of bureaucracy unnecessary. Thus, taxpayers' money is saved. The rampant corruption in most government institutions means that a long chain of bureaucracy is no safeguard against fraudulent collusion.

As we have already seen, land titles issued by governments can be easily streamlined through smart contracting. Other government functions that can be surrendered to smart contracts include a registry of births, identity management, voter registration, the voting process, granting of various licenses without favoritism, or artificial bottlenecks intended to force the public to pay bribes for hastening the transaction process.

There are many use-cases that can help boost governance. Anonymous recording of public complaints to ward off retribution, witness protection, and filing tax returns are other use-cases that governments ought to explore.

7) Supply Chain Management

With the easy availability and affordability of sophisticated technology such as Internet-of-Things, GIS, smart sensors, container scanners, among others, it is easy to track the movement of a given cargo and tell its position at any given time. Upon delivery, it is easy to verify delivery automatically.

This not only means that smart contracts can be used to convey automated updates to both managers and clients but also execute delivery transactions. If it is a logistics company that is delivering merchandise, the smart contract can make automated payments upon successful delivery.

Smart contracts can also enhance security along the supply chain by giving an instant warning when someone attempts to tamper with the cargo while still in transit. Ultimately, this reduces pilferage and fraud while improving efficiency in the management of logistics.

8) Insurance

Formulating an insurance policy relies on complex actuarial data. A smart contract that leverages Big data, Machine learning, Internet-of-Things, and Artificial Intelligence can not only be able to instantly draft a policy but also detect the occurrence of insured risk and automatically issue compensation.

For example, Big data can be used to estimate the policy value by employing the smart contract parameters. Machine learning can be used to adjust the policy value in real-time, Internet-of-Things can be used to relay signals about the occurrence of the insured risk, Artificial intelligence be used to evaluate if the insured risk thus occurred can be compensated, and the automated mechanism in the smart contract instantly releases compensation.

9) Clinical Trials

Clinical trials require an extremely high degree of confidentiality. However, the traditional methods of storing the identity of the participants and outcomes of trials are susceptible to physical or electronic hacking.

When participants' identities or test results are inadvertently released, this erodes confidence and faith in the research entities. Hence, future clinical trials become more difficult as potential participants shy away for fear of being identified and their privacy exposed.

Smart contracts not only protect participants' identities but also ensures quick authentication, seamless evaluation, and quick analysis. Feedback to participants can also be automated, thus saving the participants from the long wait and the resultant undue anxiety.

10) Escrow accounts/wallets

Probably one of the best use-cases in financial transactions, smart contracts work well with escrows. An escrow account is where the buyer and seller agree on an independent third-party account whereby the buyer deposits a certain sum of money on the condition that upon specific performance by the seller, the third party releases the money to the seller.

In traditional financial transactions, this third party is usually an intermediary bank. A smart contract replaces this third party. Instead, the smart contract has in-built escrow and a mechanism to validate the specific performance by the seller and automate the funds' release.

The advantage of smart contracts as escrows is that they are relatively cheaper, faster, and more accurate on authentication.

By employing smart contracts, blockchain escrow wallets automatically deposit and release funds based on the accomplishment of the set performance parameters.

11) Record Storage

Smart contracts can automatically store a record of transactions. We've already seen how a land registry, health records registries, voter registry, personal identification registry, among others, can be recorded and stored via smart contracts.

An active registry application is the subscription database. In this kind of scenario, the records are not just dormant; there is a regular trigger e.g., a periodic timetable for a subscription payment. A smart contract app can create periodic reminders to members, receive members' subscription fees, update the database record, and provide a statement of payment to paid members.

12) Trading Activities

Smart contracts can be effectively used in trading activities. The best-case scenario is the trading of digital products. For example, an eBook file or a music file can be delivered instantly upon the buyer paying for it. This could involve sending the buyer access keys immediately upon receipt of payment. Or the digital product getting automatically decrypted upon payment.

Physical products can also be traded using DeFi. We've already seen how land ownership can be exchanged via smart contracts. All physical products that have the title of ownership, e.g., receipt, certificate, license, permit, lease, royalty, subscription, etc., can be traded via smart contracts. This is ideal where ownership rights are strictly enforceable.

13) Blockchain rights management

Blockchain is the ideal technology for rights management due to its various features, such as immutability, transparency, and accuracy.

Some of the rights include royalty, patents, copyrights, licenses, title deeds, etc.

Some of the assets whose rights need to be managed include artwork, films, music, software, eBooks, land, mines, among others.

Smart contracts can be used to facilitate rights management functions such as royalty collection and distribution.

BLOCKCHAIN DEFI

One of the use-cases where blockchain technology has established a firm foothold is in the fintech application. Fintech has leveraged the distributed and decentralized nature of blockchain to offer financial services that would not be possible with the traditional centralized bureaucracy. Thanks to leveraging of blockchain by fintech that the world is experiencing a new form of financing – DeFi!

Decentralized Finance (DeFi)

Decentralized Finance (DeFi) refers to applications that ride on the blockchain network to deliver financial solutions to users.

Apart from the decentralized feature of blockchain, another great feature that has enabled the astronomical rise of DeFi is the concept of smart contracts. Smart contracts are a critical component of DeFi. This is why DeFi exists predominantly on blockchain networks that offer smart contract facilities. Ethereum has staked over 80% of this sector, with the rest of the blockchain networks sharing the leftovers. Why <u>Ethereum</u>? We have already discussed this earlier.

DeFi vs CeFi

DeFi is the opposite of CeFi. As you can see, the primary distinctions between the two terms are D (decentralized), and C (Centralized).

While DeFi focuses on decentralizing the financial process, CeFi focuses on centralizing the financial process. CeFi is the type of institutionalized financial framework that we are traditionally accustomed to. It is where financial transactions flow from one central authority, that is, a bank. These central authorities include Central banks, commercial banks, and financial institutions.

DeFi came about to end this centralization and hence monopolization of financial transactions by one entity to the detriment, exploitation, or cost to others that rely on it.

For example, many depositors have encountered a situation where their accounts are frozen on flimsy grounds or no grounds at all. It is also common for financial institutions to have hidden fees and also raise the existing fees without consulting their customers and depositors. Depositors are at a disadvantage when it comes to determining interest rates to earn on their deposits, while borrowers are also at a similar disadvantage when it comes to determining how much interest to pay. Most financial institutions run as a cartel under the influence of central banks. DeFi seeks to free lenders and borrowers from this cartel.

DEFI: WHY NFTS?

One crucial area where NFTs are exhibiting a strong impact is in the field of DeFi. This is because, as we shall see later, DeFi requires collateralization to succeed. NFT provides a very unique and novel form of collateralization. NFT opens up a new form of collateralization to DeFi that would have been hitherto impossible – real property. NFT being a real property or its derivative is much more stable than, say, the volatile bitcoin.

We are going to go explore more on DeFi NFTs later on.

DeFi's preferred blockchain platform: Why not Bitcoin but Ethereum?

Almost 80% of DeFi Apps run on the Ethereum platform. Why?

This is simply because of the smart contracts. Unlike Bitcoin, Ethereum was designed, from the beginning, to be a smart contracts platform.

Popular DeFi applications

Just like smart contracts, DeFi is expanding very fast in terms of use-case acreage.

The following are the primary applications of DeFi:

- **Lending platforms**: the overriding popularity in DeFi is in the field of lending. This is a field in which DeFi growth is still at the infant stage but growing very rapidly. As such, the potential is still out there.
- **Stablecoins**: stablecoins are simply those coins that are pegged to the fiat currency as a means of stabilizing the cryptocurrency exchange.
- **Decentralized Exchanges (DEXs)**: just like banks, forex entities and even money transfer entities are known to be notorious exploiters of people's hard-earned money. They also have bureaucratic bottlenecks that frustrate the transfer and exchange of currencies. DEXs allow peer-to-peer transactions. As such, if you have ethers and you want dollars, you do not need a bank or forex bureau to convert this for you. You can even exchange euros and dollars via the DEX platform using stablecoin as a go-between. The advantage of this is that it is almost instant, anonymous, and even cheaper.

- **Prediction markets**: predictive markets are multi-billion-dollar markets. Maybe it is high time we call them 'multi-billion-bitcoin' markets. DeFi, as smart contracts, can self-execute upon the happening of given future events. For example, people can bet on a certain future event. The DeFi will self-execute and automatically award the winners the agreed sum of money. No intermediary such as betting companies is required.
- **WBTC:** is a mechanism that allows users to exchange bitcoins on the Ethereum network. Since a bitcoin is just a line of encrypted code, this code can be treated as ordinary data to be further encrypted in a form that can be utilized through the DeFi mechanism.

NEW DeFi BREAKTHROUGH APPS

DeFi continues to break new grounds with creatively novel ideas. The following are some of the novel DeFi apps that are gaining ground:

- **Money Legos**: Yes, in construction engineering, we talk of prefabricated houses that are manufactured elsewhere and are brought to be assembled on site. This not only makes prefabricated houses cheaper but also extremely fast to build. Money legos follow the same principle. But, looking at it from the fun side of it, they are like toy legos that children use to construct various kinds of toys. DeFi allows you to assemble various blocks of codes to come up with the kind of financial products that you desire. Like a property developer who buys components of a prefabricated house to assemble, you do not have to do the laboriously "dirty" work of building your financial products from the ground. Simply buy the various DeFi components and quickly build your financial product for the market. The key benefit is the speed of delivery to the market.

- **Replication**: since codes for DeFi apps transparently available, anyone can replicate the existing DeFi app and customize them to unique needs. The existing DeFi app becomes a mold for crafting a new DeFi app. This reduces the time required to create a new DeFi app. You need not reinvent the wheel when it already exists. Simply find the right fit for your financial vehicle.
- **Yield farming:** This is a process whereby traders plow through a DeFi register to find those tokens that bring higher returns.
- **Liquidity mining**: This a form of yield farming where users specifically look for DeFi freebies. Yes, those free DeFi tokens. It is common for DeFi apps to offer free tokens as an onboarding enticement to potential users.

How can I mint money with DeFi?

We have already seen yield farming and liquidity farming as ways of making money on DeFi. However, the ultimate way is to use DeFi as a lending platform as intended. You can use the DeFi app to lend out your savings and earn higher interest than you would earn from your fixed deposit account.

You can actually work just as banks work – borrowing low and lending high. Thus, the margin becomes your profit.

Can I safely invest in DeFi?

DeFi investment obeys the basic economic principle of "high risk, high returns". The high return on DeFi investment is already an indicator of the high risk involved.

Being a pretty young and novel technology, DeFi has not matured to a level where it is error-free. If the app is defectively programmed, then it can burn your investment to ashes.

On the other hand, you rely on the intent of the DeFi app provider. Since there is no regulatory standard or framework for DeFi, you are the one to conduct a thorough audit as the apps are open-source. However, the biggest challenge is the technical nature of the app. You are an investor, not a coder. How do you then tell that the code is defective or won't yield the desired outcome as touted?

Just as it took some time before good cryptocurrencies crystalized on the market, it will also take some time before good DeFi apps crystalize on the market. In the meantime, you've got to be extra vigilant as far as investing in DeFi is concerned.

BLOCKCHAIN INTERNET

Most of us already know what the internet is, at least from the user's perspective.

THE BASIC DEFINITION

Internet is a global network of electronic devices.

The network simply refers to 'interconnectedness.' Thus, we can simplify this already basic definition by stating that:

Internet is a global interconnectedness of electronic devices.

WHY THIS NETWORK? WHY INTERCONNECTEDNESS?

The main objectives of this interconnectedness are:

- **To be formed into a system** – the purpose of forming a system is to collectively perform certain functions as one whole. Within the system (wholeness), protocols are created that guides the formation of sub-systems, division of functions, modalities of interaction, nature of transactions, and the means and ways of transacting, among others.
- **To interact** – the purpose of interaction between these electronic devices is to declare availability towards the purpose of the system and hence exchange information about this availability and purpose.
- **To transact** – the purpose of transacting is to exchange value. This value can be in the form of deliverables such as messages, digital products, prices, etc.

DECENTRALIZED SEARCH ENGINES & BROWSERS

Decentralized Search Engines are those search engines that run not from a central place but on blockchain network nodes.

They enjoy full features of blockchain such as democratization, anonymity, consensus mechanism, among others. Data is also fully encrypted so that no one else has access to the user data except the user herself. Since they are not run by a central authority plus other features, user data cannot be sold to advertisers, unlike Google, Bing, and similar search engines that rely on the selling of user data to profit.

The most popular decentralized search engine is Brave.

BLOCKCHAIN CMS

Content is king! This is more so the case in the digital world. For example, the internet is just like a network of bones, and the content is the flesh that makes it whole. Without content, the internet won't have much use.

Due to the large volume of content, the need to manage this content came forth in the early years of this millennium. This gave rise to the Content Management System (CMS). Currently, the most popular CMS include WordPress, Joomla, and Drupal.

However, due to the need to protect content rights and avoid falling prey to advertisement sharks and pirates that are no respecters to private rights or ownership, a need has arisen whereby these rights are protected and the publishers rewarded without compromising on their rights. Blockchain has come in handy due to its properties such as consensus mechanism, transparency, traceability (to the right owner), easy monetization, among others.

The most popular Blockchain CMS is Steemit. Steemit CMS allows publishers to earn directly from readers, thus avoiding compromises that involve advertising as a means of monetizing content.

BLOCKCHAIN IOT

Already, in our definition of the term 'Internet' we mentioned 'electronic devices'. Traditionally, as far as the internet is concerned, these electronic devices were simply computers. However, as technology advanced, not just computers were able to connect to the internet but also other electronic devices.

It is these electronic devices that are referred to as 'Things'. However, for specific use in IoT, these electronic devices have certain specific features that make them 'Things' as opposed to just 'electronic devices'.

BLOCKCHAIN THINGS

THE MAIN FEATURES OF 'THINGS.'

The following are the main features of 'Things':

1) Autonomy

This is the most important feature as it distinguishes 'Things' from other electronic devices. Autonomy means that these devices can carry out their functions independent of human intervention. This is unlike personal computers (PCs) that require someone to instruct them on what to do.

Autonomy rules out most electronic devices that rely on human intervention, such as PCs, Smartphones, etc.

2) Embeddability

Embeddability refers to the ability to embed software and sensors into the devices. It also refers to the ability of the devices themselves to be embedded into other devices.

Embeddability became important due to the smallness of most IoT devices. For example, wearables are small devices that do not have room for a hard disk or such large storage for both software and data.

3) Smart sensors

IoT devices either have sensors embedded in them or rely on sensors to execute their functions. Sensors are the signal generators that automatically provide them with data (and sometimes, instructions), that they either act upon or transmit.

SMART APPLIANCES

Smart appliances are those autonomous devices that rely on IoT to execute various functions, e.g., automatic opening of garage door, etc.

BLOCKCHAIN IOT APPLICATIONS/USE-CASES

IoT use-cases continue to expand as more enabling technologies continue to emerge. Plus, as more and more people become knowledgeable about IoT, its adoption continues to grow.

The following are the most common IoT use-cases:

1) Manufacturing

Sensors placed in critical stages in a manufacturing process can be able to detect abnormal signals and communicate the same for quick rectification before greater damage is done.

For example, if a certain part of the manufacturing process tends to overheat due to the effect of friction (which may be caused by loss of lubrication), the temperature sensor can detect abnormal heat and communicate the same to the maintenance department for action. Alternatively, this can be automated such that the temperature sensor can trigger a lubricant injector to spray or rather lubricate the affected part.

Another example is the detection of defective products in the manufacturing process. A sensor can be positioned at a certain point on the conveyor belt to detect abnormalities such as abnormal dimensions, abnormal coloration, and others. Once the defective product is detected, this information can be relayed to the quality control personnel to isolate such a product. Alternatively, in a robotic system, the sensor can trigger the robotic arm to automatically pick such a defective product and dump it into the defective product tray or defective product conveyor belt.

Another application of IoT in the manufacturing process is the use of sensors in the product or batch counting, whereby after counting a certain number of items or batches, they are taken to the packaging unit. Also, the same sensors can be used to count such that after attaining a specific number of a certain type of items manufactured, the factory can be automatically reset to start producing certain other types of items.

2) Automotive

self-driving cars are almost becoming a new norm. What makes them run on the road without a driver? IoT! Self-driving cars have dozens of sensors that help them navigate the road. Guided by the map extracted from cloud-based apps which leverage the benefit of AI and ML, these cars "drive themselves" with a much higher level of accuracy than human drivers. Of course, faults do happen, which may cause them to incur accidents that human drivers may not have incurred. But, overall, they are less prone to accidents than those cars driven by humans. Yes, they are not affected by fatigue, distraction, sluggish decision-making span, and other limitations that make us human.

Combine AI, ML, 5G, geospatial technology, improved battery power, and increased mileage of road infrastructure specifically designed for autonomous driving, the future of IoT in automobiles is bright.

Yet, automotive IoT is not just limited to autonomous driving. Fault detection and self-repair are some other IoT applications that can be utilized onboard.

3) Transportation and Logistics

Combine GIS (Geospatial Information System) with IoT, and you can track trains, ships, trucks, cars, and other assets on the move.

This ability to track assets on the move makes it easy to manage transport and logistics operations. For example, you can easily tell assets stuck in traffic and reroute them to less congested lanes or routes. You can also utilize this information to update logistic endpoints such as delivery centers (or customer centers) on the position of cargo and how long it might take to reach the endpoint.

Furthermore, this tracking can help monitor cargo on the move, such as containers. Logistics security managers can be informed in real-time when the cargo is being diverted or tampered with. Information about the state of cargo can also be relayed for prompt action. For example, the state of perishable commodities such as milk, vegetables, and sensitive pharmaceuticals, can be relayed based on data collected from the embedded sensors such as temperate sensors, humidity sensors, chemical sensors (pH sensors), pressure sensors, odor sensors, among others. This can inform managers on what to do next. The action could include disposing of such products at risk at the nearest market at a salvage value, improving the state of preservation, or other appropriate measures.

Product-as-a-Service (PaaS) business model can be molded out of this application. For example, per-use asset rental can easily be done, and thus customers pay for the use of the asset rather than a flat hire rate.

4) Retail

IoT applications can be leveraged to increase customer experience. For example, take the front-office operations whereby the IoT wearables are used to allow premium customers access a VIP lobby. Alternatively, you can have sensors that detect the queue length and thus automatically issue lane tickets to incoming visitors.

Take another example where a smart shelf has an embedded weight sensor that automatically relays information about a stock that is below the minimum level. This information can be feed to automated inventory management software, which places an order based on the set parameters for Economic Order Quantity (EOQ).

Generally, IoT applications can be utilized by retail entities to boost customer experience, manage inventory, optimize operational costs, enhance movable asset security, and increase efficiency.

5) Public Sector

IoT can greatly enhance the efficiency of G2C (Government-to-Citizen) services. For example, the government can install IoT traffic sensors on highways and use the information to alert drivers of accidents, jams, and road closures and advise them on alternative paths to take.

By the use of IoT sensors installed at various points in the water piping and distribution system, the government can be able to track water quality, water pressure, supply volumes, and leakages among others. This will enable the government to take necessary action such as improving water quality, optimize supply flow, and repair damaged pipes.

6) Healthcare

Covid-19 has proven how governments can use IoT camera sensors to track the movements of patients in quarantined zones. IoT temperature sensors installed at major public entry points such as airports, city entries, etc., can detect those with abnormally high temperatures, inform relevant health authorities and track them for testing. This has happened in China, Japan, and South Korea. The more such outbreaks continue to happen, many more governments will emulate China, Japan, and South Korea as a means of managing such epidemics. The public health safety -vs- privacy scale will continue to tilt in favor of the former.

Furthermore, IoT can be used in hospital asset management. For example, hospital management can know the exact position of IoT-embedded wheelchairs at any given time. This innovative management can save time during emergencies. The same can be the case with IoT-enabled ambulances.

Wearables are fabulous in monitoring mentally challenged patients such as those suffering from memory impairment conditions who are prone to forgetting directions and locations. They can also be used in mental health facilities to monitor mentally confused patients.

7) Safety in hazardous environments

Wearables and other body sensors can be used to monitor the safety of a given environment that is potentially hazardous. Such environments include sewer holes, mines, gas and oil fields, chemical plants, power plants, nuclear plants, among others. For example, there will be those sensors that will monitor environmental factors such as oxygen levels, radioactive levels, lighting, temperature, humidity levels, etc. Also, there will be those sensors that will monitor the body condition of those in such environments. Such body sensors include heart rate monitors, breath sensors such as carbon dioxide level sensors, among others.

BLOCKCHAIN GOVERNMENT

Government is about people, not a given central authority. In a liberal democracy, people are sovereign. People delegate their powers to their representatives (the executive, legislature, and judiciary) while retaining the sovereign right to exercise this power directly. Blockchain is the best technology to facilitate this kind of liberal democracy.

1. **Private identity rights management**

Government stores a huge amount of personal databases. To avoid duplication of data, the government can share this data with potential users, both governmental (such as immigration, police, emergency response, etc.) and non-governmental (such as hospitals, banks, insurance companies, among others. Each of the users is interested in a certain type of data.

Government can leverage the blockchain network to grant these users limited access to that portion of data that each requires. Blockchain ensures the security of this data while leveraging the distributed network to avoid the congestions characteristic of a centralized database.

Furthermore, the government can avail information anonymously such that only those with private keys can be able to identify themselves as the owners of such data while the rest may not know who the owners are. For example, data can be made public anonymously with certain aspects that would expose the identity of the person involved, such as face image, etc. is redated and only revealed to the private key holder.

2. **Citizenship management**

Apart from passports and visas, there is a lot more involved in citizenship management. For example, blockchain together with other enabling technologies such as IoT, history about a citizen's movement, current geological position, and engagement can be tracked and recorded in real-time. Of course, this will depend on existing laws regarding privacy rights.

This information can be used to track criminals, offer disaster relief to victims of catastrophe, and even allocate essential resources such as transport, foodstuff, medical supplies, among others.

3. **Voting**

Smart contracts can ensure that electorates can be elected by the people for the people so that government is what it's meant to be. A manifesto can be created through smart contracts, and only projects highlighted within the manifesto are funded, and the governors are only paid upon successful performance. Thus, using fraudulent manifestos to hoodwink the electorate to be voted becomes a thing of the past. No more promises that are not intended to be implemented.

4. **Democratization**

Democracy has been a fraud all over the globe. Even in the most established democracies, cases of **defrauding voters** are common. Defrauding voters ranges from outright rigging of votes to subtle rigging of their conscience through deceptive manifestos.

Through blockchain, the integrity of votes is guaranteed. Furthermore, voting becomes a very inexpensive undertaking such that people can vote for or against ideas at Referenda.

People can also vote out elected leaders that have veered off their manifestos.

5. **Governance participation**

Blockchain features such as consensus mechanism, continuous voting, and decentralization can allow people to participate effectively in governance. For example, through consensus mechanisms, people can vote to prioritize government projects and allocation of their taxes towards such projects.

Through decentralization and distributed system, public goods can be localized to the lowest level – the individual, without incurring huge cost-runs.

6. **Public registry**

One of the biggest functions of government is to keep the register of various public entities, including public properties, persons, maps, blueprints, among others.

Cases of some records disappearing, being hacked, or getting damaged are common, especially in the developing world. Blockchain's very strong cryptography ensures that it is hard to hack or illegally manipulate records. In case a record disappears, it is easy to replicate it almost instantly due to redundant copies being held in many nodes.

Accessibility to the public registry is the biggest bottleneck when it comes to public service. Most public services are time-restricted in terms of office hours, holidays, etc. They are also restricted by the need for extremely laborious identification procedures. These can easily be solved through blockchain. Blockchain is available around the clock – no office hours or holidays. Furthermore, by employing cryptography and smart contract features, high-security identity verification becomes automated. The blockchain's anonymity feature makes it easy to avail data to the public that cannot be easily traced to a particular person. This ensures the protection of private rights.

7. **Self-governance**

The more the citizens surrender their governance rights to a central authority, the more they cede their power and the closer they get to being oppressed.

Blockchain, by default, is a self-governance platform. It enables individuals, corporate entities, foundations, clubs, institutions, and professional associations to self-govern by providing self-management platforms that allow democratization, consensus building, delegation, and distribution of power and responsibilities.

BLOCKCHAIN IDENTITY

Identity is important not only to governments but in every transaction and interaction. It is rather hard to deal with someone who doesn't know you and has no way to verify who you are. Blockchain has contributed to making identification and identity management much easier. NFTs are slowly gaining entry into the blockchain identity business. Already sports personalities and celebrities are creating their cards that not only provide personal identity but serve as an immutable personal profile. Read <u>NFT use-cases</u> to learn more on how NFT can be utilized in blockchain identity.

The following are important blockchain identities:

1. **Personal identity**

Through blockchain registrars, that is, entities that facilitate registration and verification, you no longer need to carry loads of identity documents wherever you go. All this is securely stored online and can be accessed and verified by anyone who has an internet facility.

For example, driver's license, identity cards, social security ID, etc., can be encrypted and stored on the blockchain network. All you need is to assign whoever wants to verify your identity a one-time PIN. Once the person enters this PIN into the user interface of the blockchain network and the required information is provided. The person providing the PIN can decide how long it can be used and the type of information that can be accessed using it.

2. **Passports**

The world is increasingly becoming one global village. It is already a digital village. However, when it comes to the physical movement of people, complications still exist because we are yet to become global citizens. We are still trapped in our national jurisdictions. Thus, to move from one jurisdiction to another, you need a passport. When a passport gets lost or destroyed, it takes several days, weeks, or even months to get a replacement. This means a trip is canceled or postponed, and many opportunities are lost.

Having a blockchain passport makes it unnecessary to even carry a passport. All you need is a one-time PIN delivered to whoever wants to verify your identity and travel credentials. No more agony. No more wastage of time.

3. **Certificates**

Apart from identity documents and travel documents, certificates are important in our lives.

Some of the important certificates are birth certificate, academic/professional certificate, marriage certificate, and death certificate. There are many more certificates.

For example, when one attends an interview, the person will have several certificates that could be a dozen or more, including copies.

With blockchain, carrying all this baggage is unnecessary. All that is need to access and verify all these certificates is simply a one-time PIN.

SECURITY

One of the most important features of blockchain is security. Even though there is no system that 100% secure, blockchain achieves higher levels of security than non-blockchain systems. This is one of the reasons that blockchain has become extremely popular.

Some of the blockchain security applications include:

1. **Identity protection**

We have already discussed how blockchain can be used in the recording, storage, presentation, and verification of identity.

Two important features that make blockchain ideal for identity protection are:

- Immutability – some properties of identity or all of them can be made immutable such that no one, not even the owner of the identity, can tamper with it. Records that can be rendered immutable are those records that, once made, cannot be changed. These include birth certificates, death certificates, etc.
- Anonymity – the identity of the reference entity can be made fully anonymous.

2. **Data protection**

Blockchain data is fully encrypted in such a way that it is nearly impossible to decrypt without the decryption key. This ensures the highest level of data protection while making the very same data easily available.

3. **Network protection**

Protection of identity and data is only one side of the coin. To ensure full protection, the network that is used for the recording, storage, and transfer of data needs to be protected from malicious intrusion. For example, hackers using ransomware are not interested in reading the stored data. All they are interested in is holding the data at ransom so that you pay before allowing you access to it. Network protection will ensure that ransomware does not hold your data hostage.

Blockchain, by its consensus mechanism, anonymity, and multiple replications, ensures that ransomware becomes nearly impossible to apply. This is because even if one network node is held hostage, there are hundreds, thousands, or even millions of nodes with the very same information.

GAMING AND GAMIFICATION

People love fun. Who are you not to? The fun comes in many forms. What is funny to you may not necessarily be funny to someone else. Blockchain has made it easier to create games and gamify rather dull activities to boost performance.

The following are the main types of blockchain games and gamification

1. **Incentivization**

Some of the typical examples of blockchain incentivization applications include Steemit, ICO drops, etc.

Steemit incentivizes both publishers or content and readers of content. Publishers earn based on the number of points the content earns from readers. Readers, too, are rewarded through promotions such as 'community editor,'' community ombudsman,' etc.

ICO airdrops have been used a lot during the ICO launch to encourage participants to buy the ICOs. Airdrops simply refer to the random distribution of ICOs to participants in the ICO process.

2. **Games**

When it comes to gaming, the biggest advantage of blockchain is its distributed network. Thus, players can participate in a game across the network from diverse locations.

3. **Gambling**

In most jurisdictions, gambling is neither legal nor illegal. Yet, in stricter jurisdictions, gambling is illegal and has heavy fines and jail terms.

Both gambling sites and gambles take advantage of blockchain's anonymity and decentralized control mechanism to run gambling apps. It is difficult for government agencies to track the gambling site owners and even more difficult to trace the gamblers themselves.

BLOCKCHAIN ARTWORK

The recent addition to blockchain applications is the blockchain artwork. The most important blockchain properties that promote artwork are:

- Immutability

- Smart contracts

The most popular blockchain artwork applications are the **Non-Fungible Tokens (NFTs)**.

We are going to dwell deeper into NFTs in Part II and Part III since it is the core subject of this book.

To get started with NFTs, go to Part II.

Chapter 3

Cryptocurrency – The NFTs Power Coins

To be able to host NFTs on a blockchain network, you need to finance the mining, hosting, and exchange fees. These fees are paid via cryptocurrency. Having a basic idea of how cryptocurrencies work, how to acquire them, and the various marketplaces to buy them is important.

To be able to get a better understanding of what cryptocurrency is, it is important to not only define it but also go beyond the definition to cover its technical and financial aspects.

DEFINITION OF CRYPTOCURRENCY

We do not have a universal definition of cryptocurrency. Nonetheless, we can define cryptocurrency as a cryptographically designed and algorithmically derived virtual digital currency that runs on a decentralized blockchain network.

FEATURES OF CRYPTOCURRENCY

Features of cryptocurrency

Cryptocurrency has many features. However, we can classify these features into three main categories – technical features, financial features, and transactional features.

TECHNICAL FEATURES

- Virtual – this currency has no physical existence. It is generated by using electronic codes.
- Algorithmic – codes generated are algorithmic by nature
- Cryptic – the codes are encrypted as a guarantee of security. They also regulate the creation of new coins and verification of existing coins.
- Blockchain database – encrypted records are stored in a block.
- Decentralized – no single authority is responsible for the generation of cryptocurrencies. The cryptocurrency creation and transaction process are algorithmically driven and circulated based on peer-to-peer mechanisms. Governance decisions are made through consensus.
- Digital – traditional fiat currency is defined by a physical object such as gold, silver, etc. They are also stored in vaults. Digital currencies are not defined by any physical object but by codes. They are kept in digital wallets, which act as their store. They are transacted by transmitting them from the sender's digital wallet to the recipient's digital wallet.
- Elastic scaling – the supply of cryptocurrencies in the market scales up and down autonomously without any intervention by a central authority. This gets rid of undesired currency manipulation.
- Mining – while traditional coins are produced through a process of minting, crypto coins are produced through a process of mining.
- Open-source – the software used to create mine cryptocurrency has codes that can be readable by any software developer. Thus, developers can create their APIs

without the need to consult or seek permission from anyone.
- **Proof-of-Work** – most cryptocurrencies (Bitcoin included) rely on the proof-of-work system. In this system, a hard-to-compute but easy-to-verify puzzle is used as a way of earning the fundamental value of the coin. Thus, a token (coin) is created once a puzzle forming it is cracked (solved). Some other cryptocurrencies use Proof-of-Stake or Proof-of-State either as a substitute to or in addition to proof-of-work.

FINANCIAL FEATURES

- **A medium of exchange** – cryptocurrency works like fiat currency when it comes to exchanging value between Parties to a commercial transaction.
- **Debt-free** – like gold and other valuables, cryptocurrencies are simply virtual commodities. Unlike fiat currencies which are promissory notes, they have no debt burden.
- **Value quantifier** – cryptocurrencies can be used to quantify the value of a given worth.
- **Digitally transacted** – cryptocurrencies are transacted in digital form
- **No territorial boundaries** – cryptocurrencies are not bound by territorial borders
- **Market-driven** – cryptocurrency has no worth except that determined by the market forces of supply and demand
- **Limited supply** – unlike fiat currency, whose supply cannot be predetermined, cryptocurrencies have a limited quantity of supply that can be easily determined.
- **Value-based** – while the price of cryptocurrency is determined by the market, the intrinsic value is determined by the effort done in minting it.

TRANSACTIONAL FEATURES

- **Available in real-time across the globe** – the only time-lag incurred in the availability of cryptocurrencies is that of propagating across the global nodes. There are no bureaucratic intermediaries such as SWIFT that would cause delays.
- **Permission-less** – No one needs permission to acquire cryptocurrencies. You simply need to download the requisite software for free and use it to transact.
- **Immutable** – once a given transaction is confirmed, it cannot be reversed
- **Pseudonymous** – The real-world identities of parties to a cryptocurrency transaction cannot be established. The parties are represented by a randomly generated address code, and it is this code that becomes a visible party to the transaction. These addresses are publicly available. However, on some blockchains such as Monero, they are only available to involved parties, and thus they are also anonymous – in addition to being pseudonymous.
- *Highly secure – due to their cryptographic nature, no one can break the security framework except out of the negligence of the private key holder.*

UNDERSTANDING THE MONETARY NATURE OF CRYPTOCURRENCY

Having a monetary nature does not necessarily mean being money. It simply means performing similar functions as money. To be able to understand the monetary nature of cryptocurrency, let us answer the following basic questions:

Is Cryptocurrency a measure of value?

Yes. However, while money is a measure of an actual value of a good or service, cryptocurrency, just as fiat currency, is a measure of its virtual value. Cryptocurrency, just as fiat currency, is susceptible to speculation, inflation, and the legal, economic and political situation of the issuing entity.

Is Cryptocurrency a store of value?

Cryptocurrency, just as fiat currency, is not a store of value. For example, take the case of Bitcoin, it rose to a high of $15,000 per coin and fell to a low of $3500 per coin, all within a short duration. So, if a certain unit of gold was being tagged at $15,000 then, and later on be tagged at $3500, could we claim that this unit has been "stored" by such a currency? No. This is because, as a seller, you would have to sell four units of gold at $3500 to acquire one unit of gold at $15,000 at a different point in time. Yet, if it were a real exchange between a unit of gold and another unit of gold, you cannot give out four units to acquire 1. As such, cryptocurrency, just as fiat currency, cannot store this value of gold.

Is Cryptocurrency a medium of exchange?

Yes, just as digital fiat currency, cryptocurrency is used as a medium of exchange of value.

CAN CRYPTOCURRENCY BE USED AS A FOREX INSTRUMENT?

Yes, just as digital fiat currency, cryptocurrency can be used as a forex instrument. The only difference is that this "forex" is not based on the legal jurisdiction (such as a nation). In terms of fiat currency, forex refers to the exchange of currency of one nation with the currency of another nation. In cryptocurrency, this is simply about an exchange of one type of cryptocurrency (e.g. bitcoin) with another type of cryptocurrency (e.g. Ethereum).

However, even in fiat-based forex, cryptocurrency can be used as a medium of exchange. For example, a person can use the US dollar to buy a bitcoin and then use the bitcoin to buy the Sterling pound. As such, cryptocurrency (due to its speed, affordability, and cryptic nature) is used as a medium of exchange between various foreign fiat currency denominations.

HOW DO CRYPTOCURRENCIES WORK?

To understand how cryptocurrencies work, first of all, you need to understand the following three key concepts that underly them:

- Mining
- Public Ledger
- Transactions

MINING OF CRYPTOCURRENCY

Cryptocurrencies are simply codes that are algorithmically generated. These codes need to be validated so that they can be known to belong to the network. Validating a given code/block of cryptocurrency is what is known as 'mining.' Once mining is done, the authenticity of a given cryptocurrency is confirmed and thus authorized to be entered into a public ledger.

There are special entities (called 'nodes') that are responsible for carrying out the mining process. Miners are individuals who run the nodes. The role of miners is to secure the network by establishing that the right processes run on it and cryptocurrencies generated are genuine. This validation is carried out by special software that answers cryptographic puzzles embedded in a given block of transactions. It is only by deriving the right answer (solving the puzzle) that the validity of this block can be confirmed.

Once the puzzle is solved, the transaction is ready to be recorded into the public ledger. The cryptographic puzzles are extremely complex and require a powerful combination of processors to solve. These processors consume lots of energy to arrive at this solution. The solution provided after this process is the proof-of-work (PoW) done in confirming the validity of the transaction.

Foundational networks such as Bitcoin and Ethereum used PoW. However, as technology progresses, less resource-intensive methods such as Proof-of-Stake (PoS) and delegated Proof-of-Stake (dPoS) are being employed as substitutes. Later on, we will explore both PoS and dPoS and how they differ from PoW.

Public Ledger

A public ledger is simply a publicly available record of transactions on a blockchain network.

The public ledger records all the cryptocurrencies generated on a blockchain network and all transactions done in sequential order (block on a chain).

There is special software that handles the public ledger since it is electronic. This software is freely provided by the respective blockchain network and anyone can download and peruse it.

By making the ledger public, transparency and accountability are enhanced. This makes it possible for anyone to verify any transaction taking place and raise the alarm upon detecting any anomaly. This is also a very important security measure that discourages would-be fraudsters from creating fictitious transactions.

TRANSACTIONS

A transaction is simply an exchange of value between two parties where there is an offer and a consideration. On a blockchain network, transactions are carried out openly, and everyone can see them take place.

Once a transaction takes place, it is queued to await miners to do their work. A transaction transfers value from one wallet to another. The originating wallet encrypts a transaction with a cryptographic signature identifying it and its owner. Miners verify this cryptographic signature. Once they ascertain its authenticity, they record the transaction in the public ledger. The cryptographic signature is in the form of a mathematical puzzle that has to be computed by miners to ascertain its solution.

Each cryptographic signature is hashed to provide a public code that matches the owner's private key. Ownership of cryptocurrency recorded in the ledger as represented by the public key belongs to the private key holder. Thus, for a change of ownership to occur (that is, transfer of value), the original owner of the private key has to deliver it to the new owner. The value is then transferred to the new owner's wallet, and details are recorded in the public ledger.

HOW TO ACQUIRE CRYPTOCURRENCIES

There are several ways to get bitcoins. Mining, buying, and exchange of value (e.g., selling) are the three main dominant ways of getting bitcoins to your wallet.

1. **By mining**

Mining is the term that refers to the process of creating a bitcoin. It is a process that involves the use of a complex algorithm, dedicated network, and specialized computer facility and requires specialist skills (to get an elaborated description as to how bitcoin is mined, See 'Bitcoin Mining' herein under for further details).

2. **By selling products**

The other easy way you can get bitcoin is to sell your products and accept bitcoins as one of the alternative modes of payment. This is best achieved by selling your products online. However, you too can achieve this, albeit on a smaller scale, through a peer-to-peer exchange.

3. **By buying**

You can buy bitcoins just as you can buy dollars, pounds, or euros. You can buy bitcoins via a person-to-person exchange, bitcoin exchange networks, amongst others. However, before you buy bitcoins, you must have a Bitcoin wallet to store them.

WHY DO YOU NEED CRYPTOCURRENCY?

Cryptocurrencies are acquired for the following main reasons:

- Safe hedge – what has propelled Bitcoin is its store of value. Bitcoin has become the virtual gold standard for virtual currency. This is because, like most cryptocurrencies, their volume is known in advance.
- Speedy transaction – due to their digital nature, cryptocurrencies enable fast transaction processing.
- Low-cost transaction – cryptocurrencies use a peer-to-peer transaction process. Thus, middle agents such as banks and clearinghouses are eliminated.
- Anonymity – cryptocurrencies allow anonymous transaction processes.

CRYPTOCURRENCY EXCHANGE

There are certain specific platforms where forex takes place (e.g., Central banks, commercial banks, intermediary financial institutions, forex bureaus, etc.). Similarly, there are certain specific platforms where cryptocurrency exchange takes place. Like forex, some platforms are more popular than others in terms of volume.

The following are the ten most popular cryptocurrency exchange platforms by volume and security:

1. Binance
2. Coinbase
3. KuCoin
4. Bittrex
5. Kraken
6. BitMex
7. OKEx
8. Bitstamp
9. Bitfinex
10. Poloniex

MOST POPULAR CRYPTOCURRENCIES

There are more than one thousand cryptocurrencies in the world. However, just a few dozens of them are actively traded. The popularity of a cryptocurrency means that you can easily exchange and convert it. There is also a higher chance of it appreciating due to increased speculation. It is the speculation that makes a cryptocurrency become a more preferred investment option.

In this section, we are going to look at the five most popular cryptocurrencies in the market.

BITCOIN

Bitcoin is the most popular cryptocurrency. It is the pacesetter of other cryptocurrencies. It began actively trading since the year 2009. It was created by the anonymous pseudonym 'Satoshi Nakamoto'. It now accounts for about 45% of the entire cryptocurrency market. While there had been many failed prior attempts at cryptocurrency, Bitcoin succeeded due to its blockchain technology. The blockchain system prevented double-spending. Its early adopters were people who wanted to remain anonymous in the so-called 'dark internet' ('darknet'). These people were dealing in money laundering, hacking, illicit trade, and such other nefarious activities. However, due to the quick, less costly transaction process, it came to gain wider acceptance in terms of genuine legal transactions.

ETHER

Ether is the native currency for the Ethereum blockchain. It is represented by the 'ETH' ticker. So far, Ether is the most sought currency for NFTs due to the need for Gas utilized in the mining of NFTs.

Ether is also required for purposes of issuing ICO (Initial Currency Offering) plus other ICO incarnations that will discuss later in the book.

While more smart contracts blockchain networks have emerged, Ethereum still leads, and more than 80% of NFTs and Smart Contract Apps are hosted on the Ethereum network. This means that Ether is still the king of cryptocurrencies for smart contracts.

OTHER POPULAR CRYPTOCURRENCIES

- Ripple
- Litecoin
- Monero
- Dash
- IOTA
- NEO
- Stellar Lumens
- Zcash
- NEM (New Economy Movement)
- Cardano
- OmiseGo
- Lisk
- Tether
- Populous
- Stratis
- Hshare
- Qtum
- EOS

STABLE COINS

A stable coin is a coin whose value remains relatively fixed. To ensure this stability, this value is pegged against a non-volatile currency or asset. Most stable coins are pegged against the dollar.

Why the dollar? First of all, the dollar is considered one of the most stable fiat currencies in the world. Secondly, as a world reserve currency, the dollar is globally available. That means it has higher liquidity. Lastly, the dollar is the most recognized international currency. As such, almost all national fiat currencies are paired against the dollar in the forex market.

Thus, pegging a crypto coin against the dollar makes it gain from the many benefits of the dollar in the international currency market. Unfortunately, it also gains from some of the many disadvantages of the dollar.

Apart from the dollar, some stable coins are pegged against gold. Unlike the dollar, gold is considered true money, not just currency. Gold has been a standard of value and money long before the US came into existence long before currencies came to be used. Almost all kinds of ancient civilizations recognized gold as a measure of value. Whenever there is a global financial crisis, people rush to convert their currencies into gold. Gold is more stable than the dollar. The only disadvantage is that it is not as liquid. However, the gold's liquidity can be improved through gold derivatives. Stable coins pegged against the gold act like gold derivatives.

Bitcoin is akin to the 'gold standard' for cryptocurrencies. As such, just as some crypto coins are pegged against gold, some crypto coins are pegged against bitcoin. However, due to bitcoin's volatility, such coins can hardly be regarded as stable coins. Nonetheless, in the absence of pegging against non-crypto currency assets, they are relatively more stable than those which are not pegged. Pegging against bitcoin is more about assurance of their security (especially new coins) as opposed to their stability. Stability can be improved by pegging against a portfolio of several crypto coins (especially other stable coins) than a single volatile cryptocurrency such as bitcoin.

Why stable coins?

Those who use cryptocurrencies as a medium of exchange would like to have a currency whose value remains static for a significant period. When they price their commodity, they do not risk losses due to currency erosion. Buyers also want predictability so that when they budget to buy an item at a future date, they know how much they expect to spend.

Thus, stable coins ensure price stability in the trading market, where they are used as a medium of exchange.

Types of stable coins

Not all stable coins are equal. Stable coins are differentiated based on the underlying asset. An underlying asset is simply the asset from which a stable coin is derived or pegged to. This underlying asset acts as collateral. Those stable coins that are backed by/pegged to/derived from an underlying asset are deemed to be collateralized stable coins. Some stable coins are not collateralized and are thus termed as non-collateralized assets.

Another distinguishing factor is the protocol used to generate the stable coin (e.g., algorithm).

COLLATERALIZED STABLE COINS

The following are the three main types of collateralized stable coins:

1) Fiat-backed stable coins

These are stable coins whose underlying asset is a fiat currency. The most dominant fiat currency is the dollar.

The following are the most popular fat-backed stable coins:

- Tether (USDT)
- USD Coin (USDC)
- TrueUSD (TUSD)
- DAI
- BitCYN (BITCYN)

All the above stable coins except bitCYN are pegged to the US dollar. The first three stable coins are pegged at a ratio of 1:1 against the US dollar.

BitCYN is built on the Bitshares blockchain. Bitshares has its native coin known as BTS. Thus, bitCYN is a bitAsset (BTS) based on the Chinese Yuan (CYN). Apart from bitCYN (Yuan variant of BTS), there is bitUSD (the USD variant of BTS)and bitEUR (the Euro variant of BTS).

DAI is a unique stable coin in that it is collateralized yet algorithmically derived. It is pegged at a ratio of 1:1 to the US dollar. However, unlike other collateralized stable coins that are based on a fiat reserve, DAI is algorithmically derived by the user demand. By demand, it means that when a user takes out a loan on the MakerDAO, DAI is automatically created using a self-executing smart contract. The quantity of DAI in the market is stabilized algorithmically through the creating and burning mechanism.

2) Commodity-backed stable coins

These are stable coins whose underlying asset is a precious commodity. The most dominant commodity is gold. Oil reserves have been used or explored as a form of an underlying asset. For example, official Venezuela's cryptocurrency is based on the oil reserve.

- Digix Gold (DGX) - DGX is an example of a gold-backed stable coin that is created by the Monolith network.
- Tiberius Coin (TCX)
- SwissRealCoin (SRC)

3) Crypto-backed stable coins

These are stable coins whose underlying asset is a crypto asset or a basket of crypto assets. The most dominant

Non-collateralized stable coins (Algo-based stable coins)

Currently, non-collateralized stable coins are algorithmically derived.

These are coins whose underlying asset is derived algorithmically. The amount of coins available in the market is stabilized algorithmically through the creating and burning mechanism. Popular algorithmic stable coins include LUNA, Frax (FRAX), Empty Set Dollar (ESD), YAM, and Ampleforth (AMPL).

Hybrid stable coins

Hybrid stable coins have both collateralized and non-collateralized features. Each hybrid stable coin is unique in its hybrid protocol. Thus, it is hard to generalize them.

The following are typical examples of hybrid stable coins:

- DAI – we've already seen that DAI is a fiat-backed stable coin. This is because its nominal (face) value is pegged to the USD. However, its real value is backed by Ethereum smart contract.
- RSV (Reserve) – this is another stable coin that relies on a liquid pool of tokenized crypto assets. This pool includes stable coins such as USDC and DAI, among others.

Most Popular Stable Coins

There are dozens of stable coins out there, and new ones keep creeping up to fill this need for price stability. However, just like fiat currency, some stable coins are more widely used than others. Recognition is an important factor. People wouldn't like to trade using coins that they do not recognize or are not recognized by those that they want to trade with. The wider the recognition, the more popular a stable coin is.

The following are the five most popular stable coins:

- Tether (USDT)
- USD Coin (USDC)
- TrueUSD (TUSD)
- DAI (DAI)

Stable Coins Use-Cases

Stable coins blend the stability of international fiat currencies with the universality of cryptocurrency.

While the USD, Euro, and Yuan are pretty stable fiat currencies, they are subject to national laws and jurisdiction. They are also susceptible to the volatility of geopolitics. For example, many countries and entities have been sanctioned not to use the USD – purely based on geopolitical considerations. This has constrained their economies and damaged their international trade. The fiat currencies are also susceptible to fiat bureaucracy such as the

SWIFT system and imperialistic intermediaries such as PayPal, Skrill, and others. Cryptocurrencies came to remedy this. However, their volatility means that they cannot be a true measure of value or standardization of value. Stable coins, while offering the same remedies against fiat bureaucracy, also offer an important remedy against cryptocurrency volatility.

These important features of stable coins have brought about several use-cases. The following are the most prominent use-cases:

1. **eCommerce**

Stable coins make it easy to have fiat-free borderless e-commerce. Due to their price stability, they can be used as a standard measure of the value of the various products on the global e-commerce platform. Volatile coins such as bitcoin or Ether cannot perform such a function.

Furthermore, stable coins can easily standardize the value of a product across the globe, unlike fiat currencies that are jurisdiction-bound. For example, USD and Euro are the most popular global fiat currencies, but due to geopolitics, their availability is restricted in several countries. Above that, the US and European Union restricts their currencies from being used in certain transactions.

Also, the volatility of forex means that there is a mismatch between the value of a product in one fiat currency (e.g., USD) against the value of the same product in another currency (e.g., Euro). This mismatch and disparity can result in forex loss that can even erase the entire profit of a profit-slim product.

2. **P2P recurrent payments**

Due to their stability, stable coins can be used in contracts, especially smart contracts. This is because their future value is stable and predictable. Thus, stable coins can be used in P2P recurrent payments such as loan installments, regular salaries, standing orders, bulk payments, etc.

3. **Cross-border remittances**

The modern workforce is increasingly becoming globalized. Remote working is the new norm, especially in this age of COVID-19 and its resultant restrictions. Due to fiat bureaucracy and the high cost of currency conversion, cross-border remittances of fiat currency have become extremely expensive. Furthermore, intermediaries used are jurisdiction-bound. For example, PayPal, the most popular alternative to the expensive SWIFT system is available in less than a quarter of the world's countries. However, stable coins are available in any country that allows internet access.

It would be legally impossible for a worker in Iran and North Korea to be paid in dollars, but easy to be paid in stable coins. The ability of stable coins to overcome geopolitical barriers makes them the preferred choice of cross-border remittances.

4. Safe hedge

Places such as Zimbabwe and Venezuela have experienced hyperinflation that has gone to several million times. Currently, countries such as Iran and Turkey are experiencing volatility in their currency.

To ensure that the value of their wealth is not eroded by hyper-inflation, citizens of such countries would find it safer to sell their national currencies in favor of stable coins. In this situation, the stable coins become their safe hedge against hyper-inflation.

5. A standard measure of conversion

Like money, a stable coin works as a standard measure of conversion. For example, the value of bitcoin against Ether can hardly remain the same except in an extremely short moment. As such, if you have a certain number of bitcoins that can fetch you a certain number of equivalent value in ethers right now and you want to buy ethers three days later, the number of ethers won't be the same at the time you want to buy them. It is difficult to match two highly volatile currencies. Hence, the best way is to convert bitcoins into stable coin (e.g., USDC). You can later on use USDC to buy Ethers. In this case, USDC is used as a standard measure of conversion.

6. **DeFi transactions**

Decentralized Finance (DeFi) is here to stay. A lender would not be motivated to lend cryptocurrency worth $1000 only to receive back cryptocurrency worth $180 due to the depreciation of the value of the volatile coin used. The opposite would be the case if the borrower were to borrow $300 worth of cryptocurrency yet pay back $5000 worth of it in a month due to the sudden appreciation of the volatile coin used. This would be more about gambling than lending and borrowing.

Thus, for DeFi transactions, stable coins are the preferred mode of exchange – especially when it comes to DeFi lending. Volatile coins can be used in DeFi transactions but to greater risk exposure. In this high-risk exposure, one party will gain at the very painful expense of the other. No equal sacrifice can be expected in such a scenario.

How to store cryptocurrencies

Cryptocurrencies, just like other currencies, need to be stored before usage. Just as you keep your notes in a wallet, cryptocurrencies are also stored in a wallet.

However, the type of wallets for cryptocurrencies are digital wallets. A 'wallet' is simply an electronic file that holds digital money.

Due to the cryptographic nature of cryptocurrencies, wallets have a higher level of cryptographic security than ordinary digital wallets.

How to create the different types of wallet

You can have a wallet by;

- **Creating a local wallet** – this involves downloading and installing Bitcoin Client, which is software that you use on your computer to generate the wallet on your computer.
- **Creating a cloud wallet** – this is a wallet that resides online on a public platform such as blockchain.info.

Local wallet -vs- Cloud wallet

A local wallet is owned and possessed by you such that you have full control over it. However, unlike cloud wallets, you do run the risk of losing your bitcoins in case you lose your computer, or it gets badly damaged (or infected by a deadly virus) such that you cannot recover the data.

On the other hand, a cloud wallet, though owned by you, is not possessed by you. Therefore, you do not have full access and control over it. In case the owner of the cloud system is dishonest, you could end up losing your bitcoins. Another important risk is that of hacking. A hacker can target a cloud system and thus steal the contents of your wallet.

Whichever option you choose, it depends on how you perceive your risks. If you feel it is riskier to have a local wallet than a cloud wallet, then go for a cloud wallet. However, if you feel it is riskier to have a cloud wallet as opposed to a local wallet, simply go for a local wallet.

WARM STORAGE

Warm storage refers to storing cryptocurrencies and other crypto assets online for a short duration of time. Warm storage is supposed to be temporary since it is risky to store crypto assets online for a long duration. Apart from hacking, there is a risk that the wallet providers could cease to exist with no opportunity to reclaim your crypto assets. Warm storage is ideal for traders who just want a place to store their crypto assets temporarily pending sales.

COLD STORAGE

Cold storage refers to storing cryptocurrencies for a long duration of time. Cold storage is based on offline medium.

Cold storage is ideal for investors who desire to hold their crypto assets for long as they await an opportunity to maximize their ROI (return on investment).

The following are the main types of cold storage facilities:

1. PC Wallet – resides on the personal computer. It is mainly in the form of a folder.
2. Hardware wallet – this a stand-alone gadget created for the sole purpose of storing crypto assets. Most hardware wallets are created on highly portable dongles.
3. Ledger wallets – these are a unique kind of hardware wallets that are almost like a micro-pc. Unlike dongles, they have a screen where you can view the stored crypto assets and even manipulate them for purposes of transfer and transacting. Ledger wallets are created to suit a particular set of crypto assets, e.g., bitcoins or ethers but not both.
4. Paper wallets – The most popular kind of paper wallets are the QR Codes printed on a hard-to-tear, hard-to-wear, and hard-to-erase type of paper. As such, a QR scanner is used to read the crypto codes. The advantage of QR Codes is that the keys can be read and entered directly on the required forms for purposes of transfers or transactions.
5. Brain wallets – These are "wallets" that are etched in your memory.

PART II

INTRODUCTION TO NFTs

In this second part, we will introduce Non-Fungible Tokens (NFTs), dissect their nature, their various use-cases, and the different types.

We will show you how to convert the various types of assets at your disposal into NFTs. Further, we are going to multiple ways by which you can utilize your NFTs.

The main topics covered in this Part include:
- The nature of NFTs
- The functions of NFTs
- NFT standards
- How to turn your various assets into NFTs
- The NFT creating process
- Blockchain Networks that support NFT minting
- NFT minting platforms

Chapter 4

The Nature of NFTs

You've probably heard of NFTs. They are the new chips in town. If not yet, don't worry. We are here not only to let you know what they are but to help you make them and earn from them. Won't it be good for you to open up a new income stream? If yes, this is your opportunity to learn how. But, before then, let's start from the basics.

What are NFTs?

Non-fungible Tokens (NFTs) are unique blockchain crypto assets with the following features:

- Non-fungible – this means that they cannot be replicated or broken down into smaller units the way cryptocurrencies and other tokens are done.
- Cryptographic – their properties are highly encrypted
- Immutable – their form cannot be altered
- Exists on blockchain – Those tokens or art forms that don't exist on the blockchain are not NFTs. It is the blockchain that gives them these non-fungible properties.
- Tokenized – this, like cryptocurrencies, allows these crypto assets to be

NFT is a tamper-proof certificate of authenticity and ownership of the value of an item that lives on the blockchain.

THE ORIGIN OF NFTS

Like everything else, NFTs have their origin. The following is a brief chronology capturing the history of NFT:

2012: COLORED COINS

Colored coins were created on the Bitcoin network as a way of representing and issuing real assets via the blockchain network. Some of the assets that came to mind were:

- Company shares
- Real property
- Subscriptions
- Coupons
- Access tokens
- cryptocurrencies

However, due to the constraints of the Bitcoin network and the limitations of the consensus mechanism, Colored coins did not fair well. Colored coins were simply a very brilliant idea on the wrong network. It is important to take note that Vitalis Buterin, the founder of Ethereum, once worked on the Bitcoin project and probably this inspired him to come up with a network that could incorporate such novel ideas as Colored coins.

2014: Counterparty

Counterparty extrapolated the Counter Coin idea by incorporating meme trading and trading card game. It is through Counterparty that tradeable collectibles became a reality.

Founded by Adam Krellenstein, Robert Dermody, and Evan Wagner, Counterparty had its own crypto token XCP.

Designed as a peer-to-peer, it is an open-source financial platform; Counterparty was built as a distributed internet protocol atop the Bitcoin network.

One great feature of Counterparty is that it allowed users to create their own cryptocurrencies and similar assets.

2015: Spells of Genesis

Spells of Genesis was one of the early in-game pioneers on the Counterparty platform. The first of its kind on the blockchain. Spells of Genesis is also reputed to have pioneered the advent of ICOs through an ICO token called BitCrystals. This token was then used as the in-game currency.

2016: Force of Will

Counterparty joined hands with Force of Will to unleash more trading cards on the platform. Force of Will, being the 4th largest card company in North America by sales, was a significant entrant onto the blockchain of games. This entry by a mainstream gaming company sent strong signals into the market about the importance of blockchain.

2016: R<small>ARE</small> P<small>EPE</small>

<u>Rare Pepe Directory</u> is one of the earliest forms of meme trading that took place on the Counterparty platform. The meme was in the form of a frog character.

2017: P<small>EPERIUM</small>

In March 2017, Rare Pepe made a debut on Ethereum under the project by the name <u>Peperium</u>. This project aimed at allowing anyone to create memes on IPFS and Ethereum. It thus became the first decentralized meme marketplace and trading card game on Ethereum. Peperium had a crypto token by the ticker "RARE". The token was used to fund meme creation and listing on the trading marketplace.

2017: C<small>RYPTOPUNKS</small>

Riding on the fame of Peperium and similar projects, Matt Hall and John Watkinson created 10,000 unique characters on the Ethereum blockchain. These became the famous cryptopunks. These two creative geniuses let anyone with an Ethereum wallet claim these cryptopunks for free. They were quickly claimed and this rapidly grew into a marketplace where people bought and sold them.

The success of cryptopunks and its challenges ushered in the ERC-721 standard, which drove the NFT movement.

2017: CryptoKitties

Cryptokitties are breedable creatures that are created through playing games. They are kind of digital cats produced algorithmically such that each is 100% unique.

2017: Decentraland

Decentraland brought virtual land to the NFT world. Through Decentraland, players can buy 10 meters by 10 meters of 3D virtual space. Its massive popularity was epitomized by the raising of $26 million ICO within 30 seconds – a record-breaker in its domain.

Decentraland is a gamer's paradise. In this virtual land, gamers can explore, collect items, play games and even build their own. This brought Virtual Reality to the blockchain.

2018 - 2020: NFT market explodes!

Come 2018, the market for NFT began growing exponentially. Many NFT marketplaces such as OpenSea, RareBits, and Mintbase sprang up. Others followed suit such as Nifty Gateway, Cargo Marketplace, MakersPlace, Known Origin. And so did social NFT networks such as Creary, and Cent.

2021: NFT MAKES MAIDEN STEPS INTO THE MAINSTREAM WORLD

The year 2021 has had many big names in the real world of sports, trade, finance, etc., joining the NFT frenzy. NBA (through NBA Top Shot NFT), Twitter (via its founder's first Tweet converted into NFT), and many others. Yes, even eBay is scrambling for a share of NFT auctions! It is time for traditional fence-sitters (governments) to jump into the field. There is space for everyone.

FUNCTIONS OF NFTS

Non-fungible tokens (NFTs), by their very nature, exist to perform the following main functions:

- Derivatives – NFTs can be used to represent real assets such as artwork, real estate, etc.
- Unique identity – NFTs can be used as a unique identity for certain entities such as persons (especially celebrities), property rights, rare collections, pets, etc.,

- Memorabilia – NFTs can be used as a form of memorabilia. For example, an NFT can represent a certain historical even as captured by a certain photographer. It can be used to represent a certain sequence of steps that led to a memorable action, e.g., NBA top shot, wedding vow, etc.

TOKEN STANDARDS APPLICABLE TO NFTS

Since Ethereum is the home to more than 80% of smart tokens and more than 90% of NFTs, it follows that Ethereum sets the rules of the industry. These rules are formulated into standards.

The following are some of the standards applicable to NFTs:

ERC-20

ERC-20 is not an NFT standard. It is a standard for those tokens built on the Ethereum network. However, since the bulk of NFTs is built and hosted on the Ethereum network, it simply means that to finance the minting cost, one has to buy Ethereum-based cryptocurrencies, especially Ether. Furthermore, if one desires to raise funds through ICO (Initial Currency Offering) to fund an NFT project, it follows that such a person needs to know the ERC-20 standard.

ERC-721

This is the ultimate standard for NFTs. It provides rules and protocols for building non-fungible tokens, other assets that are not interchangeable, non-divisible, and such other properties. It also defines the metadata required to descript the ownership of such non-fungible tokens/assets. Furthermore, it defines features of personalized smart contracts for NFTs.

ERC-1155

This is a standard that largely operationalizes NFTs. It while ERC-721 is sufficient for purposes of creating NFTs, it is rigid as far as potential applications are concerned. For example, having a property that you would like to create multiple rights for, such as digital music, or an ebook, you need a protocol that allows fractionalization. ERC-1155 offers a protocol for multi-tokens, thus enabling easy trading and exchange of these tokens.

While it operationalizes NFTs for multiple use-cases, ERC-1155 is not exclusive to NFTs. It is also applicable to fungible tokens.

THE DIFFERENCE BETWEEN NFT AND CRYPTOCURRENCY

Already, by having looked at the nature of cryptocurrency and that of NFTs, it is easy to see their striking differences. Nonetheless, we can recap these differences right here:

- **Homogeneity** – cryptocurrencies are homogenous tokens. That means that one unit of a cryptocurrency is identical to

another unit of the very same cryptocurrency. On the other hand, NFTs are not homogenous. Each NFT is unique.
- **Exchangeability** – by design cryptocurrencies are a medium of exchange. Thus, one unit can be exchanged for an equivalent unit of value. Due to the uniqueness of each NFT, they are not exchangeable as each NFT has no equivalent value in another NFT.
- **Rarity** – There are millions of cryptocurrencies. Even though, unlike fiat currencies, their total number is limited, making them relatively rare, they are typically millions to even billions of identical cryptocurrency units. On the other hand, there is only one and only one NFT. As such, an NFT is extremely rare.
- **Replaceability** – since each cryptocurrency unit has almost a million equivalents, it is easy to replace the value of a lost cryptocurrency unit with another unit, even though you won't get the same public key (equivalent to a serial number of a fiat note). On the other hand, due to the rarity of an NFT, once lost, if not found, it is lost forever. An NFT is simply irreplaceable.
- **Real asset** – cryptocurrencies are not real assets. They are simply a medium of exchange. On the other hand, NFTs represent a real asset, whether tangible or intangible.

NFT USE-CASES

As we shall see later, NFT has many use-cases that have not yet been explored. Most NFT creators have rushed for the "low hanging fruits" and left the laborious task of climbing the tree to future creators.

The following are some of the "low hanging fruits" in terms of use-cases:

- Collectibles
- Art
- Music
- Fashion
- Sports
- Gaming
- Licenses and certifications
- Real asset derivatives
- Virtual world
- DeFi NFT
- Intellectual Property Rights Management
- Decentralized Domain Name Service (e.g., Ethereum Name Service)

We are going to dissect the above plus many other potential use-cases in the subsequent chapters.

ARTIST ROYALTIES

The traditional way of marketing has many leakages that make artists bleed out a lot of royalties. NFT minimizes this leakage, thus ensuring better payment to creators. Furthermore, the possibility for better recognition goes a notch higher.

Furthermore, artists rely on opaque intermediaries to sell their artwork. They cannot be certain about their earnings. Neither can they be guaranteed residual future income on the additional value that the artwork might create.

NFTs have a smart contract mechanism that ties all future earnings on secondary sales back to the creator, regardless of how long the resale chain is. Every resale can be tagged with a value that sends the specified percentage to the original creator. This ensures that the original creator gains from the ripple effect of an appreciation in value. For example, if the initial sale fetched $25 and later on skyrockets to $5 million, the creator will earn a percentage based on the $5 million rather than the original $25 as would be the case in the traditional agency arrangement.

POPULAR NFTS

Let's look at some of the popular NFTs by market value. The following are some of the NFTs that fetched insanely high price tags:

- Crypto kitties
- Twitter founder's first tweet
- Beeple
- CryptoPunks
- William Shatner's memorabilia released as a trading card
- Garbage Paid Kids trading cards by Topps
- Prospectors – a popular blockchain-based game
- Blockchain Heroes – featuring a blockchain-based likeness of famous personalities

WHAT CAN I DO WITH NFTS?

With NFTs, You can:

- Trade them in
- Stake them for passive income
- Gift your friends and loved ones
- Use them as decentralized games
- Showcase your collections profile

PROS AND CONS OF NFTS

The pros and cons of NFT vary depending on use-cases. The following are the pros and cons of art-based NFTs:

PROS

- NFTs have made it relatively easy and fast to buy and sell digital media on the internet.
- Authentication of rights and ownership of digital media has become easy, thus limited the chances of buying pirated content.
- NFTs have gamified the collection of arts and other collectibles, thus making it enjoyable.
- Efficiency
- Divisibility
- Transparency
- Authentication
- Improved artist royalties
- Reduced third-party costs

CONS

- The NFT hype has made many collectibles highly inflated.
- NFT has exposed collectibles and other forms of art to a higher risk of hacking
- Environmental concerns
- Digital wallet required
- *Young technology*

Chapter 5

What Do You Have that You Can Turn into Your Own NFT?

NFT is not an alien concept. It is not something for chosen few or exceptional people. Just because celebrities have grabbed NFTs' popularity doesn't mean it is not for all of us. You, too can create your own NFT.

What makes NFTs appear mysterious is the lack of understanding of what one can turn into an NFT. You have so much that you can turn into an NFT.

To demystify NFT, let's explore some of the common properties in your life that you can turn into NFT. These properties fall into the following main categories (not exhaustive):

- Memorabilia
- Creative artform/artwork
- Infotainment
- Journal excerpts
- Pets adoration

Memorabilia

Memorabilia refers to any collectible (object) associated with a memorable occasion. It also refers to objects kept because of their sentimental value.

Memorabilia could include a special gift, photo(s)/video/short film taken during a special occasion, something discovered or bought at a special place, etc.

Thus, memorabilia are associated with a certain occasion/event. We all have experienced important occasions in life or participated in memorable events.

Things collected or created as part of memorabilia could include mementos, souvenirs, trophies, awards, etc. It can also include writing, testimony, memoir, biography, journal, among others.

Anniversary

Anniversaries are plenty. The following are the major anniversaries that provides you with an opportunity for memorabilia:

Birthday

Every person has but only one birthday. This is a unique event that is worth remembering. The day your child is born, and activities that take place can be captured as part of the birthday memorabilia. Every birthday anniversary can be captured separated into an NFT or accumulated into a series of anniversaries that shows growth over time and be captured as one period, e.g., Childhood, Youth, Adulthood, etc.

You can turn your birthday or child's birthday memorabilia into an NFT.

GRADUATION CEREMONY

After spending days, months, and years studying, graduation is the period that caps it all. It is a moment of accomplishment, and the experience of that moment can be captured and formed into memorabilia.

WEDDING CEREMONY

Wedding happens once in a person's lifetime. Even if you wed twice or thrice or more with different partners, each wedding is unique. It is worth remembering. The event can be captured into memorabilia.

TRAVEL/TOUR

If you are a fan of traveling places, then do not let the opportunity to permanently etch your memorable travel occasions into the blockchain.

Some of the memorable travel occasions include:

1) A scenic site toured.

If you find a great scenic site, capture it! That is a great memento. Some of the scenic sites include a waterfall, forest, wild animals, panoramic skyline, among others. Differentiate it from similar captures by adding your **unique dimension,** such as your physical presence, your narrative, etc.

2) Special people, you met on your tour.

If you are good at rapport, this is an opportunity to turn it into a memento. Your encounter with a stranger is a unique moment. Capture it! You can **add value** by describing the interaction and shedding more light on the new company.

3) Cultural exposition

We have thousands of cultures. Each culture has something unique to offer humanity. As a regular traveler/tourist, you have a higher potential of exposing yourself to different and unique cultures. Grab important cultural picks, give your unique dimension and add value to it. This is a great memento.

You can bake your cultural exposition memento into a great NFT.

Events/occasions

You don't have to be an event organizer to get the best out of an event. You can turn your experience as a participant into a great memento. The rarer the event is, the greater the memento. Capture it! Give it your unique dimension and add value.

Creative Forms/Artwork

NFT is an opportunity to turn your creativity into tokens. It is an opportunity to let your creativity ride on the most unique and ever-expanding network – the blockchain network.

Fear of piracy and counterfeits plus complicated copyright and patent bureaucracy and its territorial limitations have meant that many creative minds have avoided putting their creative forms/artwork into the public domain, especially the internet.

Sad has been the experience that pirates have earned a lot more through counterfeited artworks than the inventors. Blockchain ends this sad story. It locks out pirates by ensuring that authentic pieces of art can be easily identified while counterfeits can be easily debunked.

Another sad chapter in the creative's journey has been the exploitation by the people they entrust their artwork to market on their behalf – the publishers, and label companies. Blockchain not only ends this sad story of exploitation but also opens a new door of opportunity for creatives to directly control their artworks. Through blockchain, creatives can easily distribute and monetize their artwork.

WHAT ARE SOME OF THE CREATIVE FORMS/ARTWORKS THAT CAN BE TURNED INTO NFT?

The following are some of the popular artforms/artworks that can be turned into NFT:

1. **GIF Memes**

GIF memes are by far the most popular art forms that have been converted into NFTs. If you are good at creating GIF memes that can make people laugh, then this is an opportunity for you to create and monetize your own NFTs.

Even if you are not good at creating memes, the most important thing is to have a funny idea. There are many GIF generators out there that can help formulate your idea into a meme.

Well, you can even buy memes and convert them into NFTs.

2. **Anime**

Anime is a popular art form that is used to create animated films. Anime is popular in North-East Asian countries, especially Japan and South Korea. However, they have gained wide traction across the globe.

3. Cartoons

Cartoons are popular with kids. Some adults also love them. If you are good at creating cartoons, then, this is an opportunity to make them non-fungible and tokenized.

4. Drawings

Are you good at drawing? Be it creative drawing or technical drawing. Be it a blueprint or a whiteprint. And be it a map or a polygon, there are lots of interests out there.

What more? Even if you are not good at drawing, provided you have a passion for drawing, you can buy them as collectibles and convert them into NFTs.

Again, you can hire a FREELANCE ARTIST to turn your idea into a drawing. Plenty of them exists on freelance sites such as Upwork, Fiverr, 99Designs, among others. What is important is that you own the copyrights.

5. Poems

A good poet you are? Well, don't let poor earnings discourage you. You can immortalize your poems through NFTs.

If Twitter founder earned over 2 million dollars from this: "just setting up my twttr" why not you? I bet your poem is much better than this! Yes, you can turn your poem into a monetizable NFT.

6. Articles

Do you love writing articles? Do you find it difficult to monetize your blog due to the extremely slim margins offered by advertisers? Well, NFT could be your dream come true. Why, with NFT, you will be able to kick the exploitative advertisers right in their belly. The opaque monetization algorithm by the advertisers will be a thing of the past. You will be able to craft your monetization algorithm and ride right in the pulpit of the income flow.

All you need is to write to your heart and pour in all your nuggets to craft an article of its kind. And each article in its own galaxy. Unlike with the current advertisers' monetization model, you do not have to slave yourself writing countless blogs just to attain economies of scale. No, that's not necessary. Quality, creativity, and inspiration are all that matters.

What more? No piracy. No plagiarism. Simply original. With NFT, you can keep shameless copycats at bay. Yes, outwit dream-stealers in their own game.

7. **eBooks**

The spirit of many authors has been damped by plagiarism and piracy. Copycats waiting to churn out copies of your eBook are innumerable.

But, what frustrates me the most is the case of publishers enriching themselves through your hard sweat. There is simply no accountability. For sure, you cannot tell how many copies of your eBook have been sold by the publisher or online book stores. You simply rely on faith, and a belief in what they tell you. The business of faith and beliefs is better left to religious temples. You are in business for profit!

NFT allows you to beat pirates, plagiarists, and all parasites along the chain of distribution. You are in control of your eBooks. You are fully in control of the copyrights and royalties. Other than the network cost, the entire earnings belong to you. No one else but you can skim the cream.

8. **Quotes**

Quotes are the gems of writing. If a plain tweet such as that by Twitter founder could earn millions, what about an uplifting quote? There is more to earn from it. Think about it.

9. Autobiography

Yes, you don't have to wait to be famous for writing an autobiography. This is about you sharing your life with the world in a written form. Share the much that you can. Don't look for fame; fame will find you. Simply do what you love doing with your mind, heart, and soul. The rest will fall in line.

Most famous people hardly knew that they are going to achieve the kind of fame that they got. And very few creative billionaires ever knew their invention was going to fetch billions. They simply put their all into their venture, and the rest is history. You too can.

You may think that some parts of your life are dull, painful, or shameful, but they could interest someone else, they could inspire others, and they could save a life of those who are on the edge of a cliffhanger.

10. Memoirs

Have you accomplished a mission? Yes, narrate your experience about its from start to end. It could be about your childhood, about your high school life, about your college life, about your first job, or whatever mission you engaged in and accomplished. This is your record to the world. And just like an autobiography, memoirs aren't a preserve for the famous. Simply do it!

INFOTAINMENT

Infotainment blends information with entertainment. This makes it fun to learn.

Some of the popular infotainment forms are:

EDUTAINMENT MEDIA

Though edutainment can be considered as a separate domain from infotainment, we make it a subdomain for the purposes of our exploration. Infotainment is for general knowledge, while edutainment is specifically for educational purposes and can be curated to be used in schools and other learning institutions.

Edutainment media educates and entertains at the same time.

Some common types of edutainment tools include:
- Cartoon
- Anime

INFOGRAPHICS

An infographic is a special kind of graphic that provides information in a graphic form. Pinterest is a place where many infographics are found.

Infographics are a quick way to present information in a simple yet powerful visual form.

JOURNALISTIC EXCERPTS

You don't have to be a journalist to keep a journal. Keeping a journal is a habit—one of the most important habits in life.

A JOURNAL OF AN IMPORTANT PERIOD IN YOUR LIFE

Sometimes, reviewing your journal can be quite surprising. There are quite a lot of things that you encounter in life, some thoughts that pop up, or some unique once-in-a-lifetime experience. These things may not appear such important the moment they happen. But, years later, they can be something of a wonder – a rare treasure worth sharing with others.

SPECIAL PICKS FROM YOUR JOURNAL

Extracting such excerpts from your journal and sharing them with others can give a lot of insight into important moments in your life. And probably what someone else is dying for. Such are nonfungible encounters – they will never happen again. Why not tokenize them?

Well, you can convert your journalistic excerpts into NFTs. You can choose to monetize them if you want. It is all your choice.

PETS ADORATION

Like humans, each pet is unique. It has its unique identity, not just distinguished by its appearance but also character. Pet lovers appreciate such uniqueness.

You can share stories about your pet. You can share your pet's special anniversaries with other pet lovers. You can sketch it. You can create memes about it. You can create a film about it (Remember that dog in the famous detective series?). You can make collections for it. You can prepare a journal for it. Its biography and memoir. Just think of anything that you can do for a human and find out if you can do the same for your pet. You will be surprised by the many ideas and opportunities that the pet avails to you.

And this adoration can be captured into an NFT or several NFTs. And if possible, you can monetize the NFTs. Yes, think of Crypto Kitties and such other crypto pet subjects. Think of Dogecoin and such inspirations. You aren't off-topic.

Chapter 6

How to Create Your NFT

Now, after understanding the nature of NFTs, and going through some of the ideas that you can turn into NFTs, the next logical step is to create your NFT.

THE NFT CREATING PROCESS

There is a general process for making NFT. However, in addition to the general process, each NFT minting platform has a platform-specific process depending on the type of NFT to be minted and the blockchain network that hosts the NFTs.

GENERAL PROCESS

The NFT creating process involves the following main steps:

1) Generate an idea

In the previous chapter, we have given you plenty of ideas. Yet, they are just the tip of the iceberg. You've got to be thinking. Every head has a unique idea. It is now your chance to convert that idea into an immutable form and safely distribute it on one of the most secure marketplaces – the NFTs marketplace.

2) Cast the idea into a property

With the idea in mind, the next thing is to cast it into a property. A property is simply an object with predefined features that give it utility.

Most properties that are convertible into NFT are intangible. For example, a drawing, blueprint, whitepaper, map, soundbite, music, video clip, film, GIF memes, etc.

Tangible properties can have rights associated with them that are intangible. For example, a land title deed, house lease, motor vehicle log book, etc. Intangible properties too can have intangible rights such as music copyright, business trademark, software patent, etc.

Tangible properties can also have intangible derivatives—for example, gold derivatives, etc. Intangible properties can also have their derivatives, such as crypto asset (e.g., bitcoin) derivatives.

3) Convert your property into a non-fungible art form

After casting your idea into a property, the next step is to bake the property into a non-fungible art form.

How the property is baked depends on the nature of the property and the facility used. For example, we do have various NFT minting marketplaces, with each marketplace have a set of properties that can be baked/minted into NFT. For example, a certain marketplace can be ideal for baking GIF memes, another one for baking media clips, and another one for baking a drawing, etc.

4) Publishing the NFT property on a blockchain network

To make your NFT available to the public, you have to publish it.

Each NFT is created to be published on a certain specific marketplace. For example, Ethereum-based NFT cannot be published on a Bitcoin Network or vice versa. Thus, it is important that, during the minting process, you seek a minter that is hosted on your desired blockchain network.

Ethereum network is the most popular network. As such, it should naturally come as the first choice, especially if your want to monetize your property (NFT).

5) Monetizing the NFT property (optional)

Not all NFTs are for sale. Some people create NFTs for purposes of storage on the blockchain network. Others create NFTs for purposes of sharing as freebies.

In case you desire to earn income from your NFT, then you have to monetize it.

To monetize your NFT, you need to undertake the following basic steps:

- Package your NFT as a marketable product
- Decide on the price for your NFT. Most NFTs are priced based on the highest bid. In simple terms, they are auctioned. In case you want to auction your NFT, then you will set the reserve price (minimum price)
- Promote your NFT. The marketplace's role is to make your product available to customers. However, like any shrewd businessperson, just being available in the market is not enough. You have to create awareness of your NFT through advertising. You have to attract the attention of potential customers through special offers, freebies, and other incentives. Just consider your NFT as any other digital product when it comes to promoting.
- Establish a payment mechanism. You can decide on how to be paid. You can be paid using fiat currency, cryptocurrency, or a proportion of both.
- Earn your income. Most marketplaces have a wallet where payments or earnings will be channeled. You can link your payment gateway to the wallet so that you can be able to withdraw/transfer the funds.

PLATFORM-SPECIFIC PROCESS

We are going to discuss the platform-specific minting process as we discuss the NFT Minting Marketplaces later on in the next Part.

Blockchain Networks that Support NFT minting

blockchains support the NFT token standard are also the same ones that native coins used to fund the minting cost.

To mint NFT you need to pay for network resources consumed in the minting process. Since most of the NFT minting platforms are based on Ethereum, you need to pay for GAS. Non-Ethereum-based platforms may require some other forms of resources (and coins).

The Top 10 suppliers of coins for minting NFT

Coins for minting are native to the blockchain networks on which minting takes place. The following are the Top 10 suppliers of coins for minting NFTs:

1) Ethereum
2) Binance Smart Chain
3) Flow by Dapper Labs
4) Tron
5) EOS
6) Polkadot
7) Tezos
8) Cosmos
9) WAX
10) Cardano

NFT MINTING BY PLATFORM

Almost all trading marketplaces also serve as minting platforms. The following are the top 3 minting marketplaces:

- Opensea
- Rarible
- Mintable

For more information on these minting marketplaces plus others, read "The Top 5 NFT trading marketplaces" in Chapter 8.

PART III

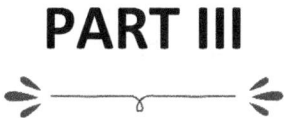

MAKING MONEY FROM NFTS

In this third and final Part, we are going to focus on how you can generate passive income from creating, trading, and investing in NFTs.

We are going to show you how to monetize your NFTs created in Part II. You will learn how to list these NFTs on the various NFT trading platforms and provide you with a detailed explanation of the Top 5 trading platforms that you can list your NFTs and how to list on each platform.

Lastly, we are going to provide you with the future outlook of NFTs so that you can be able to appreciate the future potential of NFTs and their likely challenges and opportunities.

The main topics covered in this Part include:
- Understanding the NFT tokenomics
- How to price your NFT
- The NFT trading process
- Criteria for choosing the best NFT trading marketplace

- NFT crypto investment strategy
- Lending with NFT collateral
- DeFi NFT staking
- The future of NFT, its challenges, and opportunities

Chapter 7

How to Monetize Your NFT

While it is great to create NFT for fun, there are costs involved. You need to recoup these costs. Furthermore, why not earn some income out of your endeavor?

Yes, you can have passive income generation out of your NFTs what you need is to monetize your NFT asset.

But, before monetization, you need to grasp the basic economics that drives NFT as a token and other crypto tokens in general – the tokenomics.

UNDERSTANDING THE NFT TOKENOMICS

Gaining an understanding of the NFT tokenomics will enable you to have the best monetization strategy that will result in your NFT not only being competitively priced but also awarding you optimum yield.

What determines the NFT value?

To be honest, NFT has yet to mature. As such, factors that determine its value are hardly fundamental.

The following are the key factors:

1) Sentimentalism

Sentimentalism is the determinant of the value of most NFT crypto Arts. Artwork, by its very nature, is sentimental. The value one places on it is based on one's emotional association with it.

2) Hype (FOMO)

Apart from sentimentalism, the hype is the next most important determinant. Most expensive NFTs are overhyped. People rush to buy some form of NFTs based on induced demand through advertising and the power of dark psychological marketing. Here, the heard-mentality is seized up such that one feels the "only one left out". As social beings, we feel vulnerable and abnormal when left out and thus would desire to walk with others, despite not knowing where the walk is heading to.

Through hype, an extrinsic value is created as those who are seized by fear-of-missing-out (FOMO) outcompete each other in bidding for the NFT artwork. The one whose FOMO and purchasing power blends at the highest level is the one who sets the take-away price.

While some NFTs may have fixed prices, most of them are auctioned with an underlying reserve price. The very process of auctioning raises the FOMO adrenalin within the market 'herd.'

    3) Influencers

Another crucial factor, especially for the most expensive NFTs ever sold, is the power of an influencer. The influencer could be the creator of the NFT or someone who touts it as a valuable piece of work.

For example, Twitter's founder's first tweet was sold for almost $2 million. It is a very flat and basic tweet. What made it fetch such a high price? It is nothing but the influence the Twitter founder has on the market.

The price of Dogecoin shot up exponentially simply because Elon Musk asked if Teslas customers would be happy buying Tesla cars using Dogecoins. The sharp rise in the price of Dogecoin was due to Musk's influence.

During the era of ICOs (Initial Coin Offerings), various celebrities were used as influencers to rump up the uptake of these coins, which led to the success of many ICOs.

    4) The fundamental value of the underlying asset

NFTs that act as derivatives have an underlying asset. For example, Real Estate NFTs have a real-estate property as an underlying asset. Take an example of NFT for space rental; the value of the NFT will be equivalent to the rent for space under consideration.

Another example is NFT for licensing. The value of the NFT will be equivalent to the value of the license of the property being offered.

Eventually, as NFT grows to maturity and goes mainstream, and as the legal issues get streamlined, there will be a lot of NFTs tending towards being derivatives, and hence the fundamental value of the underlying asset will become a major price determinant of NFTs in the market.

There is also a new trend where NFTs are being used as a wrapper for a portfolio of various crypto assets. The fundamental value of such NFTs is the sum value of the various crypto assets that form the wrapped portfolio.

CAN THE NFT VALUE BE INCREASED? IF YES, HOW?

Yes, the value of NFT can be increased.

This can be increased through:

1) Differentiation

Like homogenous products in the market such as salt, sugar, sweets, etc., NFT value can be increased through differentiation. Differentiation is creating a perceived difference in the mind of the consumer between two or more homogenous products such that the consumer may think that a certain product is more valuable than the other.

For example, by employing different colors of the same artwork, NFTs can be differentiated. A black and white or grey artwork may cost less than a colored artwork, etc.

2) Versioning

Like software, you can have an improved version and price it higher. The base asset (software) is the same. Each improved version can yield a new NFT.

3) Serialization

Like a movie series, you can add new series and thus price higher for the serialized NFTs. For example, a slideshow is the motion of several pictures. You can create a separate NFT for each of these pictures. You can also create an NFT that comprises several of these pictures in a slideshow for a shorter series, medium series, or a longer series, etc. The same can be done with videos, films, blueprints, maps, etc.

4) Blending

You can create several blends of NFTs. This happens when an NFT represents a formulated asset. For example, a certain recipe consists of a formulation of various ingredients. A given blend of wine can have a formulation of various sources of grapes, which can give it a unique taste. This wine can then be represented by an NFT. Each of these sources can also have its NFT. The resultant NFT is a blend. This NFT blend will have a greater value than the sum of the various NFTs that comprise it.

5) Portfolio

Portfolio is similar to blend. However, unlike blending, the assets remain independent and identifiable. It is more of a collection or assortment of various assets together.

For example, a photographer can have a portfolio comprising of various photoshoots. As such, a photo album can be considered a photographer's portfolio. An architect, a contractor, engineer, and similar professionals can have a portfolio of projects.

Similarly, an investor can have a portfolio comprising of various types of investments.

You can have NFT for each asset within a portfolio and an NFT representing the portfolio as a whole. You have the freedom to assemble your portfolio as you deem fit for pricing and marketing purposes.

Beeple sale can be considered as a portfolio that is comprised of 5,000 images. Although each image wasn't crafted as an NFT on its own, the entire collection was tokenized as a single NFT. If Beeple decided, it could have created various NFTs either for each image or a collection of several images, as it deemed fit.

6) Premium addons

Addons are common in the software world. They are also common in the assembly world. You can have a Minimum Viable Product (MVP) that meets the essential functions. However, for those who want to pay more, you can enhance the product to meet those extra functions. This helps in pricing strategy as you can meet both the needs of low-end buyers and high-end buyers without having to create different products.

Buildings, machines, automobiles, and electronic devices can also have addons.

You can create a basic NFT for the MVP and premium NFTs that incorporates the various addons, priced accordingly.

ARE NFTS SUBJECT TO THE MARKET FORCES OF SUPPLY AND DEMAND?

Yes, NFTs are subject to the market forces of supply and demand. However, unlike homogenous products, they may not be completely susceptible. On the other hand, it depends on the type of NFT. NFTs that represent pure work of art, collectibles, and rare assets do not strictly obey the laws of demand and supply, unlike NFTs that are derivatives of an underlying asset such as licenses, rentals, etc., of real estate or real property. These are just as susceptible as the real assets they represent.

CREATING YOUR NFT MARKET NICHE

Just like other marketable products, creating a niche is important. Being too thinly spread into various niches can be a disadvantage.

Creating your NFT market niche has the following advantages:

- Focused intensity: since you have a small niche, you can focus on it rather than getting distracted by generalities.
- Expertise: having a small niche to focus on can make you a most-sought expert in that niche.
- High value: due to focused intensity and depth of expertise, you can be able to create premium NFTs that can fetch a high value. This is much better than being a "jack of all trades" suffering from low-quality-low-priced burnout.

Which niche is right for you?

This is a question that only you can fully answer. However, as a rule of thumb, create a niche at that junction where your skills and passion intersect. You will never go wrong. If you are a skilled artist, go for an art-based NFT niche. If you are a financial expert, go for an investment-based NFT niche, and if you are great in interpersonal relationships such that you can create a community around you, go for a community-based NFT niche.

There is plenty of room for you to craft a niche based on your unique personality and its various assets.

Pricing your NFT

As we have seen, you can increase the value of your NFT through various forms of packaging. Accordingly, you can price each package differently.

Nonetheless, it is important to establish the basis upon which you set your price. The following are some of the bases upon which you can anchor your pricing:

1. **Based on the complete sale of ownership**

You can price your NFT upon complete sale of the asset. For example: Twitter's founder's first tweet. In this case, you forgo all rights and entitlement to the sold NFT.

The price for a complete sale is higher than that of a partial sale. You have to consider whether it is worth selling the entire NFT or some rights thereof.

2. **Based on rights**

This is emerging to be one of the most common forms of pricing. The creator of the NFT retains the right of ownership but licenses certain rights such as the right to display (e.g., Beeple), the right to play (e.g., music copyright), the right to resale (e.g., software license), etc. This is the most flexible pricing strategy. One can easily derive economies of scale by gaining the advantage of having more buyers/leases/renters while the NFTs remain affordable.

3. **Based on features/properties**

This is more about differentiation. You distinguish NFTs based on features/properties. For example, selling a photo as black-and-white at a lower price and as colored at a premium price. It can also include the use of MVP and premium products.

4. **Based on pieces/parts/fractions/shards, etc.**

Fractionalized NFTs (F-NFTs) are becoming common due to the extreme prices. For example, the Beeple that sold for $69 million and the tweet that sold for $2.9 million are examples of expensive NFTs that would not find easy buyers.

There are those expensive NFTs that may not fetch a high price because they have no sentimental value or do not reside within the hype bubble. Such NFTs, especially for real assets, may not attract huge attention. To boost their liquidity or ease of purchase, fractionalizing or sharding them becomes the best option. This often happens in the financial world when a company goes public through IPO. The value of the company is simply fractionated into smaller denominations so that they can be easily bought on the Securities exchange. This is the case with NFT sharding.

Some artists have fractionalized their artwork through various NFTs based on a part of the artwork such as drawing, or parts of a film, etc.

In case you have an NFT that is taking a long time to sell, or you suspect it may take a long time to sell, then the best option is to fractionalize it and price each piece separately.

Chapter 8

Trading in NFTs

As commodities, albeit virtual, NFTs can be traded in just as one can trade in other commodities such as precious metals (e.g., gold, silver, platinum, etc.), oil, among others.

Just as NFTs obey ordinary commodity investment rules, they also obey ordinary commodity trading rules.

THE NFT TRADING PROCESS

1. Know the trading marketplaces available to you
2. Choose the right trading marketplace
3. Join your preferred trading marketplace
4. Open the NFT wallet
5. Fund your wallet
6. Buy the NFTs that you want to trade in
7. Sell the profitable NFTs
8. Hone your trading practice

THE TOP 5 NFT TRADING MARKETPLACES AVAILABLE TO YOU

Here we are going to look at the trading marketplaces that suit a variety of NFTs. While NBA Top Spot, CryptoPunks, Auxie

Infinity, and Decentraland outperform some of the Top 5 NFT trading marketplaces listed here in terms of sales volume, they lack the kind of mix that would attract a general trader.

1. **OpenSea**

Opensea is the largest digital marketplace in terms of NFTs. It offers a wide range of crypto art assets and domain names. More than 700 projects are hosted on Opensea. Furthermore, Opensea allows more than 240 payment methods thus catering to a wide variety of customers and traders. Opensea interface is also user-friendly hence making it easy for beginners.

Self-listing is the natural phenomenon of Opensea's user-friendly interface. Opensea is to NFTs what Uniswap is to cryptocurrencies. On this platform, one can trade/swap NFTs from various other platforms, including most of the Top 6 platforms mentioned herein.

Opensea is easy to use, such that artists just need to input basic information such as Name, Category, and type of data (mutable and immutable). Immediately after the NFT is created, it is automatically listed. You don't need to know how to code to create an NFT. Simply click on the "Create" tab, and your NFT is minted and listed.

The biggest advantage of Opensea is that it is a marketplace where you can sell your NFTs created elsewhere. This is because Opensea is compatible with open blockchain standards.

The use of smart contracts means that your asset doesn't have to be held hostage on the platform. Instead, your assets are held in the wallet which is connected to Opensea, as it can also be connected to other platforms.

With over 200 categories of digital assets, you can't miss a category to place in your asset. This is why over 400 million NFTs are on Opensea. For traders, this is a huge collection of assets to trade in. If you an NFTs trader, you are spoilt for choice.

KEY FEATURES

1) Blockchain network

Ethereum.

2) Supported file types

The following are the supported files that you can upload to be converted into NFT:

- Images
- Video
- Audio
- 3D Models

3) Types of tokens traded

- Collectibles – some of the famous collectibles on Opensea include Cryptokitties, Joyworld Joys, unisocks, and Axie infinity. Most of these collectibles have had tremendous success. For example, a pair of unisocks started trading at $12 per pair, now each pair goes for about $76,000. YouTube video collectibles can also be minted. Among the famous YouTube videos to be minted include Certified Justin Kan Stories. Justin Kan is the founder of the Twitch platform that was sold to Amazon at almost $1 billion.
- Virtual cards – popular virtual cards on Opensea include Decentraland and Sominum Space. These are tokenized virtual spaces that exist in virtual reality. Apart from virtual space, games are also sold, including Sandbox products and the Zed Run's virtual horses.
- Art – Hash marks is the leading art collection on Opensea, with more than 16,000 digital portraits. Waifusion is another art collection on Opensea that has thousands of anime-inspired artworks. Waifusion is exclusively on this platform. 'NFT Yourself' by Kings of Leon is another success story of an album that sold for over $2 million. This price included 18 Golden Tickets to the album's events. Markerspace and SuperRare (marketplaces in their own regard) also have special boats on Opensea.
- Sports – Sorare tokens are among the most popular sporting NFTs. Other notable sports cards include The Global Fantasy football with its 126+ football clubs and Animoca Brands with its F1 tokens. Racing, golf, and other sporting tokens are popular on Opensea.
- Trading cards – Gods Unchained is among the popular digital cards on Opensea. Trading cards can be sold at a fixed price, auctioned, or even offered for free.
- Domain names – Ethereum Name Service (ENS) is the leading decentralized domain names registrar. Opensea provides an opportunity for one to buy domain names from ENS.
- Utility – Polyient games, POAP, and Urbit ID are among the popular providers of utility tokens on Opensea. Utility

tokens provide features that can be unlocked in the future. This allows buyers of such tokens to fund whitepapers that end up in projects. They are a kind of replacement for the famous ICOs.

4) Listing options

Opensea has one of the widest selections of listings. This allows sellers to optimize their returns and buyers to have a wide base to choose their best options. The following are the listing options available on Opensea:

- **Highest-bid auctions**: This is the best option when you are not sure about how to price your NFT yet you do not want to discourage buyers with an expensive price. Neither do you want to lose the opportunity to fetch the best market price. In this option, you select the highest bidder for your NFT. To make sure that you do not lose on the deal, you can place a reserve price.
- **Fixed-price**: this is an option that allows the seller to place a non-negotiable price on the item to be sold. Nonetheless, you can still accept a lower price at your discretion. By fixed price, you get to choose the currency denomination and even the validity period to which the price is applicable.
- **Bidding without listing**: for hot NFTs, it is possible to get a bid even before listing. You can opt to net these early offers. However, make sure that you do not sacrifice better opportunities that may be availed through the listing.
- **Declining price**: in this option, the start price is higher than the end price. In addition to setting the start and end prices, the seller also sets the duration of decline. Whoever bids at the right price along the declining plane as algorithmically determined wins the bid.

5) Compatible wallets

- MetaMask
- Trust
- Coinbase
- Bitski
- Authereum
- Fortmatic
- Arkane
- Dapper
- Argent

Plus, many more

    6) Payment method

More than 240 payment methods.

    7) Charges

2.5% on sales charged to the buyer.

OTHER FEATURES:

- Multiplatform integration
- Bundling up to 15 NFTs
- Referral program: 2.5% on sale from those referred.

EARNING OPPORTUNITY

- Sales
- Royalty
- Referral commission

IDEAL FOR (TARGET MARKET)

- Collectors who seek a variety of NFTs
- Beginners looking to learn more about digital collectibles
- Traders who want to buy and sell several types of NFTs

Pros & Cons

Pros

- Wide range of assets
- Opportunity to trade in custom NFTs and NFT bundles
- Highly configurable and customizable auctions
- No gas fees for creators until the NFT sells
- Low fees & gas free transactions
- Strong reputation and corporate backing
- Competitive commissions
- User-friendly interface
- You don't need coding knowledge to mint NFTs. This makes it easy to establish your NFT collection without the need for technical know-how
- No fee charges for creating NFTs. Only charged for sales.
- Available on iOS app
- Industry-standard security that allows secure login
- Secured by smart contracts which makes fraudulent transactions almost impossible.

Cons

- Limited customer support. However, this is understandable bearing in mind that the platform is automated, and trading is anonymous.
- You must have a crypto wallet to be able to create and trade in NFTs
- Does not accept transactions in fiat currencies

Social Media Profiles

- *Telegram*
- *Discord*
- *Twitter*
- *Instagram*

- *Facebook*

CONCLUSION

Opensea is not only the leading NFT marketplace but also a kind of supermarket for other markets. Other marketplaces such as Rarible, CryptoPunks, and Auxie Infinity have also been listed on Opensea. This ensures that Opensea has the widest collection of NFTs.

2. **Rarible**

Launched in early 2020, Rarible boasts of a sizeable collection of digital artwork and memes. Being user-friendly, open-source, and operating on a consensus mechanism has enabled it to climb the ladder extremely fast to command this enviable position. Users do not need any coding knowledge to create NFTs.

By offering its digital currency, RARI, Rarible has not only made it easier for users of the platform to fund their projects but also vote on core issues of concern. RARI is not just for funding operations on the platform but also acts as a governance token. Being a governance token, one can use it for staking.

Rarible has collaborated with Opensea such that there is cross-listing at the very same fee of 2.5%. This has virtually expanded the marketplace, thus giving both creators and traders a bigger market for their NFTs and other crypto arts.

Among artists and celebrities who have found Rarible their home include actress Linsey Lohan, rappers Mike Shinoda and Soulja Boy, billionaire Marc Cuban, among others.

KEY FEATURES

1) Blockchain network

Ethereum.

2) Supported file types
- PNG
- GIF
- WEBP
- MP4
- MP3

Maximum file size: 40 MB

3) Types of tokens traded
- Punks and Memes – CryptoPunks are the most significant punks ever traded on the Rarible marketplace. They have fetched a whopping $2 million due to their scarcity and limited supply. When it comes to memes, the Nyan cat meme is the most successful of its category. It fetched 300 ethers with an equivalent fiat value of $590,000.
- Photography and Art – Beeple is so far the most successful photography album ever sold on Rarible, which fetched a record-breaking $69 million. Other pieces of art range from Pest supply to Murat Pak. Anything from Logos to 3D can be uploaded on Rarible, tokenized, and monetized.
- Music – both audio and video files can be uploaded on Rarible and minted. This enables musicians to have control over their products. The benefit of this is that musicians can

decide how to monetize their products and how to distribute the various rights associated with their products.
- Metaverses – metaverses are shared and distributed virtual spaces. These metaverses can exist on multiple networks, multiple marketplaces, and shared by multiple entities. Decentraland is a typical example of a metaverse.
- Games – NFTs monetize digital games in ways that would have otherwise not been considered possible. For example, various assets that form a game such as avatars, skins, swords, etc. can be tokenized and monetized as separate items such that a player will need to acquire each of these assets and formulate a game. The NFT gaming industry is rapidly expanding. Rarible has seized this opportunity by collaborating with MyCroptoHeroes to increase gaming assets on this marketplace.
- DeFi – Rarible provides an opportunity for NFT-backed DeFi. Wrapped crypto NFTs can be traded on this platform.
- Domains – decentralized domains are the future of the smart internet. Ethereum Name Service (ENS) was the first decentralized domain registrar to utilize the power of blockchain smart contracts. Binance Smart Chain domain has extended this facility to new levels. Rarible provides a marketplace where decentralized domains can be bought.

4) Compatible wallets

Ethereum-based wallets such as:

- Metamask
- Fortmatic
- Coinbase Wallet
- MyEtherWallet
- WalletConnect

5) Payment method

Cryptocurrency only. Ethereum only.

6) Charges

Both the buyer and the seller are charged 2.5% each. That is, effectively, a 5% fee.

EARNING OPPORTUNITY

- Sales
- Royalty

IDEAL FOR (TARGET MARKET) [FOCUS]

Rarible is an ideal platform for self-listing. This allows a great diversity of NFTs, including collectibles, digital art, trading cards, among others.

HOW TO OPEN AN ACCOUNT

Opening an account on Rarible is quite easy. The following are the basic steps to follow:

1) Create a compatible Ethereum-based wallet (e.g., Metamask).
2) On the Rarible platform, connect your wallet. Once connected, the platform will generate your account automatically. You will have immediate access to your account once auto-created
3) Click on 'My Account' to personalize it to your taste. Personalization includes the display name, profile picture, custom URL, and a brief bio. Confirm the personalization by clicking on 'Update Profile'.
4) In case you need a verified badge, fill in the Typeform under the FAQs page. A verified badge is created after you provide details that can prove your authenticity and that of your products.

HOW TO CREATE AND SELL NFTS

With an account already opened:

1) Go to the top right of the page and click the "CREATE" button
2) Select minting a Single NFT or NFT with multiple editions/copies
3) Upload your asset to be tokenized, e.g., music file, video, or image.
4) Input properties of your file such as format, file size, or metadata.
5) Fill in the required/relevant information. This includes name, description, price, royalties, etc. Without inputting the price, the created asset will go into an auction for bidding.
6) Click on the 'CREATE' item.
7) Upon prompt, sign in to your wallet and pay the requisite gas fee
8) Optionally, consider the 'unlock once purchased' feature. This will allow buyers to have access to digital keys, URLs, and discount codes, among others.
9) Confirm the transaction upon prompt.
10) Sign the sell order once the token is minted
11) You can now find your minted NFT under 'Collectibles.'

PROS & CONS

Rarible, like any other platform, has its pros and cons that you need to weigh.

Pros

- Easy-to-use user-friendly interface
- Easy to mint new NFTS
- Native governance token – RARI
- Non-custodial marketplace

- No coding experience required to create NFTs
- Solid investor backing
- Specialized for digital arts
- Open-source codebase and protocol
- Plenty of community discussion platforms with active community
- Low-cost peer-to-peer trading
- Availability of earning opportunities via secondary sales (royalties)

Cons

- No IPFS storage or API
- No mobile app
- Neither roadmap nor whitepaper exists to provide the platform's future direction
- Scanty FAQs and contact details
- Limited customer support
- High minting cost due to expensive gas fee
- Requires external crypto wallet
- Confined to Ethereum blockchain network

SOCIAL MEDIA PROFILES

- *Telegram*
- *Discord*
- *Twitter*
- *Instagram*

CONCLUSION

Rarible has quickly gained prominence as one of the top-most NFT marketplaces dedicated to artists. It is one of the few community-governed NFT marketplaces where holders of the governance token (RARI) have a say about key decisions regarding the direction of the platform. The platform allows leveraging the NFTs for DeFi staking. Raible's partnership with Opensea has expanded the market for NFTs hosted on it, thus exposing NFT creators to immense market opportunities. Its creative innovation has attracted a huge base of renowned celebrities, giving it the desired market endorsement. However, due to its extreme liberals, it has also attracted high-end scammers, thus scaring away the risk-averse creators.

3. **SuperRare**

SuperRare is a non-custodial decentralized social networking marketplace for art collectors and creators.

SuperRare takes security to a high level by requiring thorough authentication of artists to make sure that they own the artwork or collection that they want to list.

Through smart contracts, while collectors and traders may earn from sales, royalties go straight to the original creators of the artwork.

KEY FEATURES

1) Blockchain network Ethereum.

2) Supported file types

- Images (JPEG, PNG, GIF)
- Video (MP4)
- Audio
- 3D Models

Maximum file size: 50 MB

3) Types of tokens traded

SuperRare is mainly for art collections.

4) Listing options

Creators have the option to set a fixed selling price for their NFT or set it up for auction. Once sold, the NFT can be resold. However, royalty accrued from resale is channeled back to the creator while the reseller fetches the sale price.

5) Compatible wallets
- Metamask
- Coinbase wallet
- Nexo wallet
- Several other Ethereum-based wallets

6) Payment method

Cryptocurrency only. No debit/credit cards. No PayPal. Only Ether.

7) Charges

SuperRare has various charges. An artist pays a 15% gallery fee to list the artwork. The buyer of the artwork pays a 3% fee of the artwork price.

In the secondary market, the creator earns 10% royalty for every secondary sale.

While 15% is extremely high in the NFT marketplace, compared to the physical art galleries, this is competitively low as it is normal for conventional art galleries to charge as high as 50% or more.

The creator also pays gas fees which range between $0.5 and $2 worth of Ethers per piece.

OTHER FEATURES:

Social collecting – SuperRare bills itself as a social platform where art lovers **connect and collect**. Thus, the act of buying art collections is deemed as "social collecting". Artists and collectors interact around their shared passion – the collectibles. Focusing on this social aspect, the platform provides details of top collectors, how many pieces they have bought, and how much gas they have spent. It also provides details of trending artists, how many pieces they have created, and how much gas they have accumulated. The purpose of these details is to inspire following and add vitriol to social discussions.

EARNING OPPORTUNITY

- Sales – for the first sale, creators earn 85% commission on sales.
- Royalty – creators receive a commission on secondary sales

The smart contract system tracks sales and earnings, thus letting original creators of the artwork earn royalties (commission on resale prices). The royalty earning is automated via smart code.

IDEAL FOR (TARGET MARKET)

While it is possible to set a fixed sales price for an NFT, the SuperRare platform is ideal for auctions. It is also ideal for social art collections.

HOW TO BUY NFTS

The following are the main steps to follow to buy an NFT on the SuperRare marketplace:

1) Open an Ethereum wallet. MetaMask is preferred. Follow the instructions required to secure your wallet.
2) Deposit some cryptos (Ethers) that you will use to buy the NFT
3) Connect your wallet (using your wallet address) to the SuperRare, and the account will be auto-created
4) Update your profile by providing your username, email, and other personal details
5) Email your wallet address to the SuperRare team to be whitelisted so that you can trade in NFTs.
6) Select your artwork for purchase and buy it. You will be prompted to approve the purchase via MetaMask. Once approved, you become the new owner of the artwork on the Ethereum network.

How to Bid for an NFT

After going through the first five steps of "How to buy NFTs" highlighted above, you are now ready to start bidding for NFTs. Many pieces of art on SuperRare do not have a set price and thus available for auction.

After scrolling through the artworks on display and reaching the one that attracts your interest, click on it. If it has a bid option, click on 'bid.' You will then place your bid price. If your bid price becomes the highest, you win. Many artworks have both 'buy' and 'bid' options.

How to Create NFT for Sale

You can sell artwork either as an original creator or a trader. Whichever the case, the following basic steps will lead you to a successful sale:

1) Set the metadata, including name, description, tags (at least one but not exceeding ten), and the number of copies to sell.
2) Review details for correctness since once minted the tokens cannot be edited.
3) Click on 'Issue Token'
4) Click on the three boxes of terms to agree
5) Click on "Begin Tokenization"
6) A pop-up screen will appear showing the Ethereum blockchain transaction, total price in ETH, set item price, and confirmation prompt.
7) Click on "Confirm" to create the NFT token for sale

8) In about five minutes, the token will have propagated on the network and displayed on your Profile. Once listed on your profile, the NFT is available for sale
9) Collectors can now follow the "How to Buy" steps to purchase your listed NFT.

PROS & CONS

SuperRare has its pros and cons. The following are the main pros and cons of this platform:

Pros
- Automated royalty earnings
- Connect and collect social mechanism

Cons
- High listing fees
- Complex authentication and verification process

SOCIAL MEDIA PROFILES

- *Telegram*
- *Twitter*
- *Instagram*

CONCLUSION

SuperRare is the go-to place for famous artists and celebrities. As such, rigorous verification of artworks and artists is done to ascertain the authenticity of the work submitted and the parties involved.

The socialization component is great and allows artists and collectors not only to have an important following but also makes it easier for them to market their wares.

4. **Nifty Gateway**

Unlike most NFT marketplaces, Nifty Gateway is a centralized marketplace. Furthermore, it is one of the few NFT marketplaces that accept fiat currencies in the transaction process. This makes it easy for those who would not have otherwise been able to access cryptocurrencies to participate in the creation and trading of NFTs.

Nifty Gateway is owned by Gemini LLC, an already very successful cryptocurrency exchange owned by the Winklevoss brothers. Thus, it is already backed up by a very reputable background and established on a strong technical and financial foundation.

Arts and collectibles on the Nifty Gateway marketplace are known as "Nifties." This marketplace blends arts and crypto-technology to come up with a wide variety of unique crypto assets that expands the trade and investment avenues. Each collection on this platform is known as "drop" and is listed for sale at a specific time for a defined duration. Currently, the marketplace targets to release a new drop every third week until reaching a billion drops.

Nifty Gateway is the home of stars and celebs. It boasts of such names as Grimes, a Canadian musician who fetched $6 million from the marketplace after selling her virtual artworks. Apart from Grimes, other popular musicians and artists include Carl Cox, Lil Yachty, Ozuna, Gramatik, Deadmau5, 3LAU, Mad Dog Jones, John Burgerman, Genies, Greg Mike, Justin Roiland (Co-Creator of Adult Swim's Rick and Morty), Matt Gondek, Lushsux, among many others. Kobe Briant and Mesut Ozil are also represented through murals. Beeple is also featured on this platform with record-breaking $69 million sales. We can't forget Trevor Jones and his captivating collection of moving pieces under the Bitcoin Angel artwork label, the 'Mankind'. The list of famous artists, musicians, players, and celebrities is just impeccable.

Being centralized, the music and artworks are carefully selected and curated by the platform's team of experts.

KEY FEATURES

1) Blockchain network

Ethereum blockchain network.

2) Listing options

The following are the possible listing options on the Nifty Gateway platform:

- Global offer – This is an offer provided by a buyer to the entire network of creative owners. The buyer simply submits the offer to all creators, and any of them willing to sell at that price will do so.
- Open edition – this is a temporary listing period that lasts between 5 minutes and 15 minutes. During this period, an unlimited number of NFTs on the selected piece are availed. Potentially, thousands of NFTs could be sold.
- Drawing – in this listing, a given NFT is placed in a raffle or lottery. The winner of the lottery gets the chance to buy the desired NFT for the indicated price. It is typical for thousands of entrants to participate in the prized lottery. Drawing has been necessitated by the desire to outsmart bots.
- Silent auction – in this listing option, sellers place a 'blind' bid and wait to see whether they have won.

3) Compatible wallets

MetaMask is the only wallet allowed.

How to deposit NFTs into Nifty Gateway from an external wallet

If you have NFTs that you would like to trade on the Nifty Gateway that are on wallets other than the MetaMask, the following are basic steps on how to do it:

1) Connect to MetaMask Wallet – this is the only wallet allowed.
2) Confirm that you are the owner of the wallet – select 'verify ownership' in the account info and you will be channeled to the verification page. Fill in the required information to get verified. Without being verified, you cannot make a deposit.

3) Transfer the NFTs - Once verified; you can now transfer the NFTs from the verified wallet to the Nifty Gateway wallet. Simply go to the Deposit Nifty page and transfer your NFT into the connected Nifty Gateway wallet. Confirm the transfer.

4) Payment method

Nifty Gateway is one of the very few NFT marketplaces that allow you to use fiat currency via Debit or Credit card to buy NFTs.

Cash-Out: You can withdraw your money after sales or refund to your US bank account or even to your Debit/Credit Card. However, this facility is only available in the US. Outside the US, you can withdraw to a Gemini account and from this account withdraw to your local bank. There is a maximum cash-out limit of $5000 per week when withdrawing directly. However, this limit is not imposed when withdrawing via a Gemini account. Thus, even if you are in the US, if you want to beat this limit, then the trick is to use your Gemini account.

For US customers, the following are the withdrawal procedures:

1) Log in to your account on Niftygateway.com
2) Visit the 'balance' page
3) Provide your bank details
4) Verify that your bank information is accurate
5) Select Cash Out to Bank option

The withdrawal process begins immediately and can take up to 5 days

For non-US customers, the following are the withdrawal procedures:

1) Log in to your account on Niftygateway.com
2) Visit the 'balance' page
3) Add your Gemini Account to your bank details
4) Submit your account to verification.
5) Once verified, select the Cash-out option and fill in the required details
6) Confirm the transaction

5) Charges

Nifty Gateway takes 5% of the sales price plus 30 cents transaction fee. Those making resale have to part with 10%, which goes to the original creators. Thus, if you are a reseller, you have to factor in all these charges, which equate to 15% plus 30 cents transaction fee.

EARNING OPPORTUNITY

- Sales
- Royalty
- Referral commission

IDEAL FOR (TARGET MARKET) /FOCUS AREA/WHAT IS THIS MARKETPLACE IDEAL FOR?

Nifty Gateway is more about digital arts. Nonetheless, other forms of collections can be found.

HOW TO CREATE NFTS

Unlike the above-mentioned platforms, creating NFTs on Nifty Gateway is not straightforward. You require to make an application through the 8-part questionnaire form. You are also required to successfully undergo a rigorous interview process.

HOW TO BUY NFTS

If you are an art collector or trader, you need to buy NFTs for your purpose. The following basic steps will lead you to a successful purchase:

1) Open a Nifty Gateway account by clicking on the 'Sign Up' button available on the home page.
2) Enter the required personal details and create a username.
3) Fund your account – you can either use Fiat currency or ETH. Alternatively, you can go straight to the market and pick the NFT you are interested in buying. You will be prompted to enter the payment details.

HOW TO SELL NFTS

With MetaMask wallet, selling NFTs on Nifty Gateway is a straightforward process. This process involves the following few steps:

1) Get to your Nifty Gateway account.
2) Access your wallet. Select the NFT that you want to sell
3) Set its price and click on 'Put on Sale'. This will create a wallet transaction
4) Send the wallet transaction to your Nifty Gateway account for approval and onward sale
5) Once the approval is confirmed by the system, the NFT will be listed for sale

PROS & CONS

Nifty Gateway has its pros and cons. The following are the main ones:

Pros
- Exclusivity – The vigor with which the Nifty Gateway team vets the NFT artists and picks on the best ensures that its artists are exclusive, not the type that you can easily find everywhere else.
- Unique collections – due to having exclusive artists, Nifty Gateway boasts unique collections that are hardly found elsewhere.

Cons

Restricted bank withdrawal – direct bank withdrawals from Nifty Gateway platforms are exclusively for US bank account holders only. Those who do not have US bank accounts have to navigate to the Gemini blockchain exchange, which is a great inconvenience.

Hacking history – The famous 'NFT heist' happened on Nifty Gateway where many accounts were hacked and thousands of dollars worth of NFTs stolen. Even though this was due to negligence on account holders' part as a result of failure to utilize the 2FA mechanism, the marketplace still suffered reputational damage.

SOCIAL MEDIA PROFILES
- *Discord*

- *Twitter*
- *Instagram*

CONCLUSION

Nifty Gateway is a place to get exclusive artwork. It is the best place to get NFT for long-term investment. It is also a great marketplace for high-end NFT traders who would like to fetch premium margins on their trades due to the exclusive collections.

5. BakerySwap

BakerySwap is probably the most DeFi-centric NFT marketplace today. It offers most of the typical features that you would find on a DeFi marketplace, such as Uniswap. These features include Automated Market-Making (AMM), an important DEX feature.

BakerySwap is a pacesetter in its niche, the NFT Finance (NFTfi). It is the first NFTfi hosted on the Binance Smart Chain (BSC). BSC has become popular due to its efficiency, affordability, and high liquidity – the very challenges that Ethereum currently faces. BSC's rapid growth is likely going to eclipse Ethereum in the not-so-distant future – unless Ethereum quickly recalibrates its growth engine.

Ridding on the BSC's modern engine, BakerySwap is assured of a brighter future as a pioneer in its niche.

THE BAKERYSWAP DEFI EXCHANGE

BakerySwap's AMM DEX leverages the BSC's wide array of crypto assets to offer DeFi liquidity pools.

Users can stake their various crypto assets on BakerySwap and Binance and in exchange, receive Liquidity Provider tokens (LPT). The providers of liquidity to a given pool earn a trading fee in proportion to the ratio of their LPTs in the pool.

LPT holders can easily redeem their initial crypto assets based on the conditions set in the smart contracts. It can either be automatic or upon demand.

BAKE is the native token on BakerySwap. It is not only used to mind NFT meals, it can also be staked.

TO ADD LIQUIDITY TO A POOL

To add liquidity to a pool:

1) Click on 'Exchange' on the top menu
2) Select the 'Pool' tab
3) Click on the 'Add Liquidity' button
4) Select the pair of tokens that you want to liquidate. For example, the most popular token pair is the BAKE-BNB pair. If you select BAKE-BNB pair, you will receive a BLP (Bake Liquidity Pool) token
5) Go to 'Earnings' and choose a matching option to your BLP token. The options are in NFTs e.g., Waffle.
6) Key in the value of tokens you desire to stake
7) Confirm your choice
8) Upon confirmation, the baking process begins. After a while, you will start earning BAKEs.

TO REDEEM YOUR STAKED TOKENS

Simply unstake your BLB tokens. Alternatively, click on the 'Harvest' button to manually collect your BAKEs.

KEY FEATURES

1) Blockchain network

Binance Smart Chain (BSC).

2) Supported file types
- Images (jpg or png)

The image requirement is size not more than 10m, 3:4 ratio, and .jpg or .png format.

Types of tokens traded

BakerySwap, being an NFTfi platform, allows most of ERC-20, and BEP-20 (Binance equivalent of ERC-20) tokens to be traded on. Most tokens that can be staked on a typical DeFi platform can also be paired with BAKE as stakes.

3) Listing (baking) options (pools)

As an NFTfi platform, baking is the primary activity. Various goods can be baked such as Rolls, Doughnuts, Croissant, waffles, etc. Each of these baked goods forms a liquidity pool. Each bakery pool has its unique return on investment (ROI).

Like an ordinary diet that is an assortment of various ingredients, bakery pools are an assortment of various "ingredients". In BakerySwap terminology, these are called NFT Combos. Like cakes, their worth is based not only on the ingredients but also the sizes. Taking an example of a cake, the sizes could be branded as small cake, medium cake, large cake, etc., with each having its price tag. However, BakerySwap has unique labeling of its NFT Combos.

Primarily, there are four types of NFT Combos:

- Basic: 10,000–20,000 BAKE
- Regular: 20,000–50,000 BAKE
- Luxury: 50,000–100,000 BAKE
- Supreme: Above 100,000 BAKE

The Staking Power varies depending on the amount of BAKE you have staked and an algorithmic multiplier.

4) Compatible wallets
- Metamask
- WalletConnect

5) Payment method

You can either use BNB or ETH to stake. You can easily convert ETH to BNB or BAKE on the platform.

6) Charges

BakerySwap charges are based on the AMM model whereby 0.25% goes to the liquidity provider while 0.05% goes to the bake holders, thus making up a gross of 0.3% transaction fee.

Being a DAO (Decentralized Autonomous Organization), BakerySwap is maintained by a group of anonymous developers who earn one BAKE per every 100 BAKEs farmed. Compared to traditional minting or GAS on Ethereum, this is an extremely low rate.

How to Start Baking

1) Go to the BakerySwap *site*
2) Login to MetaMask to connect to BSC by clicking on 'Settings' and changing the network name to 'Binance Smart Chain'
3) In the RPC URL space, input '*https://bsc-dataseed1.binance.org/*', enter 56 as ChainID, select BNB symbol, and use '*https://bscscan.com/*' as point locator for the block explorer.
4) Buy BNB on Binance and transfer it to the wallet. On the withdrawal page, select 'BEP20'
5) Provide your wallet's BEP20 address so that BNP can be loaded into it
6) Enter the Bakery and choose whether to 'Swap or Pool'
7) In case you want to swap, choose your trading pair and click on 'Swap'. Confirm the transaction on MetaMask.
8) In case you want to pool, specify the number of tokens you want to add to the liquidity pool. Click on 'Supply' and confirm the transaction on MetaMask.

Now you have your Bakery Liquidity Pool Tokens. Enjoy your baking.

Farming BAKE

Farming BAKE is about browsing for the best earning opportunities on the 'farm' (marketplace) and grabbing it. In the farming process, you select a token pair with the best yield, add it to the liquidity pool and stake it for earnings.

THE BAKERY NFT SUPERMARKET

This is the place where NFTs are traded on the BakerySwap.

BSC Artist' Feature

In addition to NFT Combo, BakerySwap functions like other NFT marketplaces through its BSC artist' feature. The NFT supermarket has a collection of Binance NFT, BSC artist's profiles, and a host of other digital artworks. Some of the popular artistic assets include pet eggs, battle pets, game arsenals, etc. There are also plenty of virtual artworks.

As a supermarket, it is a marketplace for artists all over the world who bring their virtual artwork for exhibition and sale.

How to display your artwork on the Bakery NFT supermarket

1) Go to the *NFT Supermarket page*.
2) Click on the 'Mint Artworks' button.
3) Fill in the required details in the provided form, including:
    - Your name
    - Artwork's name

- Your profile link (social media or website)
- Description of your artwork
4) Upload the artwork's image by clicking on the '+' sign in the upload window
5) Tick on the Copyright T&C
6) Click on the 'Mint' button
7) Wait for approval
8) Upon approval, set the price (optional) to list your work on the NFT Supermarket.

You can always view your artwork by clicking on the 'My Artwork' button on the BSC Artist Page.

HOW TO BUY NFT COMBO

You can buy NFT Combo just like any other NFTs. NFT Combo is also available at the NFT Supermarket.

The following steps will guarantee you purchase of your preferred NFT Combo:

1) Visit *BakerySwap site*
2) Connect to BSC network
3) Click on 'NFT Supermarket' on the BakerySwap site. BakerySwap Combo will appear below the site.
4) Ascertain that you have enough BAKEs to buy your desired Combo
5) Buy and way for the Supermarket team to approve. Upon approval, your NFT will be endowed to your custody
6) Ascertain the staking power of your Combo and farm appropriately
7) Upon earnings, your BAKEs and Staking Power will be shown in the 'My Combos' section of your profile
8) Approve NFT BLP for farming by using one of your Combos by clicking on the 'Approve Food BLB' button

Steps (1) to (5) are also applicable to buying other types of Bakery NFTs. Steps (6) to (9) are specifically for yield farming, of which only Combos can be used.

DECOMPOSING NFT COMBOS

BakerySwap has a decompose function that breaks Combo NFTs back to their original elements. This is an exceptional advantage over ordinary ERC721 tokens.

Decomposing NFTs allow the holders to reclaim 90% of the original worth rather than disposing them at a throw-away price.

COMBO STAKING POWER

Combo Staking power is raised by a multiplier factor. The multiplier factor is determined by the system's algorithm. You can typically get 10x for high-value Combos.

The formula for Combo Staking Power is as follows:

$CSP = rFX * B$

Where;

CSP = Combo Staking Power

rFX = Random Multiplier Factor (auto-generated when composing the Combo)

B = the value of BAKE contributed toward composing the Combo

BETH Liquidity Mining on BakerySwap

Ethereum 2.0 is expected to bring efficiency while significantly lowering mining costs. However, due to its requirement that one has to stake a minimum of 32 ETH, to become a validator, many potential validators are already discouraged.

The good news is that Binance has a cheaper alternative in the form of BETH. BETH is available on both the Binance Smart Chain and Ethereum Blockchain. The beauty of BETH is that it grants users 100% on-chain staking income. This is the cheapest gateway to ETH 2.0 for validators.

Currently, BETH is exclusively available on BakerySwap. There are three liquidity pools paired with BETH. These include:

- BETH-ETH
- BETH-BUSD
- BETH-BNB

EARNING OPPORTUNITY

- Sales
- Royalty
- Referral commission

IDEAL FOR (TARGET MARKET)

- Collectors who seek a variety of NFTs
- Beginners looking to learn more about digital collectibles
- Traders who want to buy and sell several types of NFTs

SOCIAL MEDIA PROFILES

- *Telegram*
- *Twitter*

CONCLUSION

BakerySwap is a pacesetter when it comes to marriage between NFTs and DeFi. Furthermore, it is a pioneer of its kind on the Binance Smart Chain. With BakerySwap, art meets finance. There is NFT art for artists and NFT Combo for financiers. You can be both or either. And either way, BakerySwap meets your needs. BakerySwap is where art meets taste.

CRITERIA FOR CHOOSING THE BEST TRADING MARKETPLACE

The following are criteria that will enable you to choose the best trading platform for your NFTs:

- Safety – how safe is the server and its website?
- Liquidity – how much and fast is the cash flow?
- Fees and spread – how much fee is being charged per transaction?
- Transparency – how transparent is the exchange in terms of prices, volumes and coins transacted?
- Means of payment – what means of payment are available (for both buying and receiving sales proceeds)?

- Customer support – is customer support good? Are customers happy? How fast and effective are customer issues being handled? What are the common customer complaints?
- Reputation – what is the current rating of the trading platform?
- Beginner-friendliness – is the platform friendly for beginners? Does it have sufficient resources to help beginners learn how to trade on its platform? Does it offer dummy accounts where beginners can practice before being skilled enough to trade on the platform?

HOW TO OPEN A METAMASK WALLET TO KEEP YOUR NFTS

MetaMask appears to be a must-have wallet for most NFT platforms. This makes it imperative to learn more about it.

MetaMask supports most ERC standards, including the ERC-20, ERC-721, and ERC-1155. As such, it is the most preferred wallet for Ethereum-based marketplaces. Given that most NFT marketplaces are Ethereum-based (including Binance Smart Chain), then MetaMask is an obvious natural choice. Furthermore, some blockchain networks use Solidity programming language, such as the Tron blockchain network. This makes them compatible with the MetaMask wallet.

MetaMask itself is a dApp that is hosted on the Ethereum network. As such, it is a wallet that is native to Ethereum. This makes it easy to utilize crypto assets stored in it on Ethereum-based marketplaces.

HOW TO INSTALL METAMASK?

MetaMask exists as a browser add-on and is available in <u>Chrome Web Store</u> and as a <u>Firefox Add-on</u>.

Steps:

1) Install the MetaMask browser add-on
2) Click on the 'Create a Wallet' button
3) Craft a strong password for your wallet
4) You will be provided with a seed phrase. Back it up. This phrase will be used to recover your password once forgotten.
5) Confirm back-up for the wallet setup to complete

In case you uninstall the MetaMask add-on, you can always re-install it and open the wallet by providing the seed phrase.

Chapter 9

Investing in NFTs

NFTs are virtual commodities and can be invested in just as investment in other commodities such as precious metals (e.g., gold, silver, platinum, etc.), oil, among others.

Like other investments, you can establish a portfolio of various investments. They obey all the rules of investments, including risks and returns.

VARIOUS TYPES OF NFT-BACKED CRYPTO ASSETS TO INVEST IN

Different experts categorize crypto assets differently. Due to their unique nature and recency, their true picture is yet to fully unveil.

In this book, we will categorize crypto-assets into the following main types:

- Cryptocurrencies – these are crypto assets used in the encryption, regulation, and verification of transfer of funds. We do have native cryptocurrencies and non-native cryptocurrencies. Native cryptocurrencies are those that are

created, hosted, and traded on a particular platform, e.g., bitcoin, ether, etc. Non-native cryptocurrencies are those that are platform-independent.
- Tokens – these are crypto-assets intended to fund projects, compensate service providers, or facilitate decision-making. Though not intended, some are used like cryptocurrencies. They include utility tokens, security tokens, governance tokens, etc.)
- Derivatives (pegged to an underlying asset, e.g., stable coins, futures contracts, call options, etc.)
- Collectibles (artistic value in the crypto form, e.g., crypto kitties and other forms of non-fungible tokens)

NFT-CRYPTO INVESTMENT STRATEGY

NFT is not only great collateral but also a great form of leverage when it comes to investment. The advantage of NFT being capable of representing real assets makes it the best leverage for investing in crypto assets.

Using NFT to invest in crypto assets requires a sound investment strategy. While each investor is unique and thus will come up with their own investing strategy, there are still general investing strategies considered by most investors.

Common strategies include:

- Unbalanced Portfolio
- Balanced Portfolio
- Profit re-investing
- Dollar-cost averaging

UNBALANCED PORTFOLIO

In the unbalanced portfolio strategy, you allocate your investment to each investment item (vehicle) based on how much weight you give it. You allocate the highest percentage of your investment to the item you consider to bear greater weight in terms of projected returns or performance.

The following is a sample of allocation using the unbalanced portfolio

- Bitcoin (40%)
- Ether (30%)
- XRP (15%)
- Monero (10%)
- DASH (5%)

An unbalanced portfolio is for seasoned investors who can make an in-depth analysis that enables them to forecast and project the potential of each investment item.

BALANCED PORTFOLIO

In the balanced portfolio strategy, you simply shortlist your best investment items. Once you shortlist them, you spread your investment evenly across the items.

For example, if you have shortlisted 5 investment items and your portfolio fund is $7,500, you may spread it as follows:

- Bitcoin ($1500)
- Ether ($1500)
- XRP ($1500)
- Monero ($1500)
- DASH ($1500)

Any increase in your investment fund will be automatically spread evenly to these investment items (vehicles).

A balanced portfolio is ideal for those who have no time to make an in-depth analysis of the market performance of each investment vehicle to get to the bottom of its fundamental value. It is also ideal for newcomers into the investment market or those who lack the advanced technical know-how to establish the fundamental value of a given investment vehicle or its long-term market value based on trend analysis.

Profit Reinvesting

Profit reinvesting is a strategy where you plow back the profit of your investment into your portfolio but on new investment vehicles. This way, you can expand your portfolio without risking a new principal investment.

Depending on whether you are a risk-taker, risk-neutral, or risk-averse, you will determine how much percentage of your profit you are going to reinvest. A risk-taker may reinvest more than 50%

of the profits, risk-neutral just about 50%, and risk-averse below 30%. Generally, profit reinvesting is for the risk-averse who do not want to risk new money from their pockets.

Dollar-Cost Averaging

In this strategy, you invest a fixed amount of dollar (or any other currency) into an investment item at regular intervals.

Dollar-Cost Averaging is ideal when you have a long-term projection of the crypto assets you want to invest in such that you are not bothered by short-term swings.

This strategy attracts passive investors who cannot follow the performance of crypto assets frequently.

Indicators of NFT-backed long-term value of crypto assets

One of the most important things to a long-term investor is the long-term value of a given investment. While you cannot establish with certainty the long-term value of a given crypto-asset investment, the following are key indicators to watch out for:

1. **Market share**

Market share refers to the percentage of market capitalization that a given crypto asset has relative to the rest of the market. If this market share becomes persistent in its trend, then that is a solid crypto asset. You can make a long-term investment depending on whether you just want to secure your investment away from other more volatile investments (in case of a horizontal trend) or you want to have long-term gain (in case of an upward trend). So far, Bitcoins control above 50% of the market share.

2. **Utility**

Utility refers to the ability of a given crypto asset to satisfy the wants of the market. A crypto-asset with a higher utility will attract more demand and hence greater value in the long-term as opposed to a one with low utility. For example, bitcoin may have high utility for gold-standard investors while Ether may have higher utility for Smart Contract creators. On the other hand, IDO (Initial Dex Offering) may have higher utility for those interested in the DeFi business.

3. **Transaction volume**

Transaction volume may indicate the liquidity of given crypto assets. Crypto assets that experiences very high volume of transactions means that it has higher liquidity than a one that experiences low volume of trade. Liquidity is extremely important since it is an indicator that the investor will be able to find a market for his crypto-assets should he decide to dispose of it off.

A long-term bullish volume means that the crypto asset has an appreciable long-term value. This is an indicator of a solid investment.

4. **Technological development**

Crypto assets have no other value except that derived from their unique technology. A technologically advanced crypto asset makes it become increasingly adopted, become the leader of other crypto assets, and the standard benchmark. Thus, a crypto asset that keeps on churning new technological breakthroughs (in terms of mining, transacting, and storage) means that it has a long-term future value.

5. **Market sentiments**

Market sentiments are extremely important in a market that experiences a high level of volatility such as the crypto-assets market.

Crypto assets are extremely volatile than most other assets. A change in market sentiment can grossly affect the market value of given crypto assets.

If the market sentiment about a given crypto asset has held positively consistent for a significant period, then, that crypto asset has a great future potential as a long-term investment. On the other hand, if a certain crypto asset has held a consistently pessimistic market sentiment, its prospect as a long-term investment is dim.

RISK-VS-RETURN CONSIDERATION FOR NFT-BACKED CRYPTO ASSETS INVESTMENTS

Risk is an inevitable factor of any given investment. The higher the risk, the higher the returns. The lower the risk, the lower the return. Crypto assets such as bitcoin have endowed investors with some of the most obscene gains ever witnessed in recent times. Yet, the very same investment has eroded some other investors off their value in the most corrosive way. While bitcoin has created some billionaires, it has converted some millionaires into paupers. The difference being in the timing of when to invest and when to harvest the returns.

While bitcoin has been volatile, there have been less volatile cryptocurrencies such as stable coins. Profits due to investing in stable coins are just as slim as those of investing in fiat currencies – but much slimmer due to blockchain mining and transaction costs. A risk-seeker would jump into the strong see-saw wave of bitcoin while a risk-averse investor would walk along the flat plain of stable coins.

The difference is in balancing between one's appetite for gain and fear of pain. We've already seen how risk-taker, risk-neutral, and risk-averse investors make their investment strategies. The same is the case with NFTs. NFTs obey the investment law.

Thus, like other investments, you have to make the risk-vs-return considerations in establishing your desired portfolio.

Some NFT investments can be worth millions of dollars right now and be worth a dime a few years ahead. Yet, some NFT investments can be worth a dime now and worth millions a few years ahead. Yes, bitcoin was once less than $1 and a few years later hit over $60,000. At times it has tumbled down from a cliff of $15,000 to the bottom of $3,000 in a period of a few weeks, thus causing tears to short-term investors who had no holding power but to pull out at a loss.

Investments are like that. But, shrewd long-term investors can overcome the emotional shocks of short-term swings in the market.

The Advantages of Long-term NFT-backed Investment

A long-term investment is not for everyone. Even if one has the will to invest long-term, without the power to do so, it isn't possible. The power to invest long-term depends on how long you can set aside your funds without pressure to consume it. Thus, long-term investors have the advantage of having funds that are not for immediate or short-term use. They can wait and be patient for months and even years.

Long-term investors are marathoners of the investment race. If you are a sprinter in the investment race with no stamina for long-term endurance, don't attempt the marathon because you will quit along the way. Evaluate your financial stamina.

While sprints (day-trading) and other short-term investments have their advantages, they also have disadvantages that can be effectively cured by the marathons. Marathons, too have their disadvantages.

Let's just look at some of the advantages of long-term NFT-backed investment (NFT marathoners).

The following are the major advantages:
- Lower transaction fees – due to less turnover, long-term investments consume less transaction cost. This is unlike traders (short-term investors) who have to buy and dispose of their investment several times. Withdrawing and re-investing are costly and extremely costly on gas fees. If not careful, transaction costs can easily wipe out any potential profit margin pushing the short-term investor into the loss territory.
- Less risk – the urgency does not push long-term investors to withdraw such that they end up being forced to withdraw

at the low tides. They can patiently wait for the high tide and withdraw at a bigger profit margin then. This makes their investment relatively risky compared to short-term investors, even though both types of investors hold the same asset.

- Fewer resources consumed in the analysis – short-term investors have to keep on analyzing the market. The shorter the investment, the more analytical resources are consumed. For example, an investor who has to withdraw and re-invest within every sixmonths will spend a lot of analytical resources compared to an investor who has the opportunity to withdraw and re-invest once n 5-years. The initial cost of analysis by the long-term investor is potentially going to higher than the initial cost of analysis by the short-term investor. However, every new cycle of analysis by the short-term investor increases the cost that could end up being several times more than that incurred by the long-term investor.
- Potentially higher returns – most investments give a higher rate of returns to long-term investors than to short-term investors. Staking is one such investment in the NFTfi. The longer you stake, the higher the rate you will be offered on most NFTfi marketplaces. Furthermore, you are likely going to earn bonuses and dividends in the form of 'airdrops' and similar freebies.

INVESTMENT OFFERINGS THAT CAN LEVERAGE NFT ASSETS

1. **ICO (Initial Currency Offering) – The precursor to NFTfi**

Financially, an ICO is simply an offer by a creator of a project to take a stake in its future. Technically, an ICO is simply a crypto token.

There are two types of ICOs:

- UTO (Utility Token Offering) - is a form of funding where the provider of UTO receives funds via the sale of the UTO to finance an underlying project. By buying the UTO, the investor buys a stake in the proposed project.
- STO (Security Token Offering) – is a form of an offer to access rights to a given resource. NFTs are modeled on the STO.

2. **IEX (Initial Exchange Offering)**

IEX is a form of ICO that is offered by the cryptocurrency exchange platform as opposed to its users. It is less risky as it is guaranteed by the existence of the platform as opposed to an unknown individual who is not accountable to the investors.

Axie Infinity (AXS) and Band Protocol (BAND) are two famous NFT marketplaces that utilized the EIX on Binance Launchpad to successfully establish a platform.

3. **IDO (Initial DEX Offering)**

IDO is an extension of IEX specifically applicable to Decentralized Exchanges. It a way for businesses to tap into DeFi liquidity pools by offering tokens to fund various projects including NFT projects. It is a low-cost, quick, and safer alternative to ICOs since the project creator does not own equity in the project to have controlling interests that may be used to the detriment of the investors.

4. **INO (Initial NFT Offering)**

INO draws a lot of its features from ICOs. However, it is specifically tailored for NFTs. Capcom and NBA are among the top corporates to offer INO. Entrepreneurs such as Gary Vaynerchuk (founder of VaynerX) and Jack Dorsey (founder of Twitter) also made INO.

INO is simply offering NFT to the public for the first time.

5. **ISNO (Initial Stake NFT Offering)**

ISNO is an extension of INO. However, in the ISNO, the creator offers a limited edition of stackable NFTs for sale.

ISNO can be staked on an NFTfi platform to provide a host of specified rewards much similar to those due to staking other crypto assets plus more creative rewards.

Torum is the pioneer of ISNO.

NFT Stocks for Investment

One way to invest in NFT is not to buy the NFTs but invest in stocks of companies that deal in NFTs. It is similar to investing in companies that deal in gold rather than investing in gold itself.

The main advantage of this is that you are investing in the experts who run the properties rather than exposing yourself to the risk of investing in the wrong property. This is the best option for those who are risk-averse or too busy to be involved in the technical aspects of dealing with an assortment of properties.

This is also the easiest way to diversify your NFT investment portfolio without spreading thin due to limited funds. The stocks are already diversified on your behalf.

Factors to consider before investing in an NFT stock entity:

- Technical trading signals: Since you are investing in the stocks of an entity dealing in NFTs rather than NFT, your analysis of the performance of a given stock is the same as the analysis of any other stock on the securities exchange. You are more of a securities investor rather than an NFT investor.
- History of association with NFTs. The entity that deals in NFTs must have a reputable record both in terms of NFT investment and financial reputation.
- *The extent of NFT exposure: The entity you want to invest in its stock should be deeply invested in NFTs. The NFT should be the most significant portfolio of its investment. Furthermore, it should be directly involved in the NFT*

process, either in creating, hosting, marketing, or trading in NFT or a combination of several of these or all of them. The more the entity is exposed, the greater the interest, focus, and expertise.

Chapter 10

NFT-Based Lending and Staking

NFT has become one of the most important crypto assets in the DeFi world. It has enhanced DeFi as far as collateralization is concerned. Soon, NFT will become the de facto standard of DeFi collateralization. This is going to be achieved as <u>NFT goes mainstream</u> in the near future.

<u>Improved standardization</u> and <u>minimizing scams</u> are the prerequisites for NFT becoming the de facto collateral for DeFi.

Nonetheless, the DeFi world is not waiting. It has embraced NFT wholeheartedly and both are going to grow stronger and walk together like the Siamese twins of the fintech journey. There is just a lot of potential for NFT in the fintech. In this chapter, we are going to explore how NFT is being utilized in the DeFi, especially with regard to lending, borrowing, and staking.

Lending with NFT Collateral

Lending and borrowing cryptos has become a very popular trade. In just about 3 years, this sector has grown exponentially such that it is nearing $1 billion in terms of loans issued. The biggest challenge with lending and borrowing cryptos has been having stable collateral. The high volatility of cryptocurrencies such as bitcoin has meant that sometimes the collateral is 200% the value of borrowed funds. This is understandable, given the extreme and highly rapid swings in the market value of bitcoin and established cryptocurrencies.

Stable coins have been used as a form of collateral. However, they aren't as popular as bitcoin. Nonetheless, they have improved the stability of DeFi collaterals. Add NFT and this greatly improves the collateral options.

Given that DeFi is still a very young fintech sector, competition is not yet established. It is still not yet stiff. With stiff competition, the margin of collateral requirements will go down. DeFi is also yet to go mainstream like many commercial banks and traditional lending institutions. The future is bright, going by the already exponential growth in the DeFi sector.

What motivates someone to lend with NFT?

Unlike cryptocurrencies, NFTs can represent real assets. Thus, there is greater security in genuine NFTs as opposed to volatile cryptocurrencies.

The primary driver of lending cryptos is to gain interest income without sacrificing capital gains. Cryptos have shown the tendency to create **exponential capital gains** that, unlike traditional loans, one wouldn't wish to risk losing such gains. For example, it is not unheard of for a crypto investment to yield a capital gain that 100 times or even 1000 times the value of an investment within a short span.

Thus, while waiting for capital gains to accumulate, there is no need to let such an asset remain idle. What better way than to lend it? This is the gist of it.

What motivates someone to borrow with NFT?

Borrowing with NFTs can result in cheaper loans due to NFT being capable of representing real assets. Unlike cryptocurrencies that are highly volatile and not backed up by any tangible assets, NFTs can be backed up by real tangible assets such as land, buildings, gold, machinery, equipment, company shares, and such other real-world assets.

The closer an NFT represents a real asset the lower will be the risk of volatility. The lower the risk of volatility the lower will be the margin of collateral required—furthermore, the lower the risk, the lower the interest rates. Thus, NFT-backed loans are more likely to be less costly compared to cryptocurrency-backed loans.

Unlike traditional borrowing, borrowing cryptos or fiat currency is secured against NFTs. Then, why would someone offer NFTs as security for crypto loans instead of simply selling the NFTs? Again, the primary motivator desire not to lose the likelihood of earning **exponential capital gains.** Thus, when you use your NFTs as collateral, you do not lose on the capital gains. But, when you sell your cryptos, you sacrifice this potential to earn capital gains.

Thus, unlike traditional lending and borrowing, the key motivator that drives NFT-backed crypto lending and crypto borrowing is the need to preserve **capital gains.**

PARTIES TO NFT LENDING

For NFT-Backed lending to happen, three parties have to be involved:

    1) The lender

The lender is the individual investor who provides funds that can be borrowed using NFT collateral. Most of these investors hold crypto assets intending to receive capital gain from the cryptos appreciation. Meanwhile, instead of their crypto assets laying idle, they decide to lend them out to also receive passive income.

2) The borrower

The borrowers are those individuals seeking funds to finance their projects. The project could be personal or business or a combination of both. Borrowers use their NFT as collateral for their borrowing. Whether to borrow fiat or crypto depends on whether the platform allows borrowing cryptos in addition to fiat currency.

3) The exchange platform (NFT lending platform)

The NFT lending platforms are the loans marketplaces where lenders and borrowers meet to exchange value using NFT collaterals.

NFT LENDING PLATFORMS

There are two main types of crypto lending platforms – the CeFi lending platform and the DeFi lending platform.

CeFi Lending Platforms

CeFi lending platforms operate more or less like a bank as far as centralized services are concerned with the exception that the collateral for loans is in crypto form. The loan products can be either in fiat or crypto, depending on the particular platform.

The main distinction between CeFi and DeFi is the know-your-customer (KYC) requirements. Compared to DeFi, CeFi has the following pros and cons:

Pros;

- Secure – since CeFi employs the KYC policy, they weed out unscrupulous characters who intend on committing fraud on the platform.
- Margin lending
- Higher returns to investors compared to DeFi platforms
- Beginner-friendly as there is human support. Human support means you can get proper advice when need be. This is especially important when you want to find the best options to diversify your investment portfolio

Cons;

- Strict KYC requirements can discourage or turn away potential investors
- The use of third-party agents who handle the verification of KYC requirements and for loan approvals wears down the privacy protection in addition to the extra delays in the approval process

Some of the popular CeFi crypto lending platforms include:

- HodlNaut
- Celsius Network
- BlockFi

It must be noted that, unlike the DeFi lending platforms, CeFi lending platforms have hardly adopted NFTs as collateral. However, this trend is likely going to change in the near future.

DeFi Lending Platforms

Decentralized Finance (DeFi) has brought new and immense opportunities in the finance sector. Borrowing, lending, and investing are the three critical components of finance. DeFi has taken up these components with great vigor.

DeFi lending is a revolutionary DeFi mechanism that allows borrowers and lenders to interact without the need for traditional intermediaries – a primary characteristic of the CeFi mechanism. Governments, banks, financial institutions – their bureaucracies and exploitations are done away with. Instead, borrowers and lenders interact directly via a peer-to-peer (P2P) mechanism. Apart from network costs, lenders get the full profit of their sacrifice without their gain being siphoned off by intermediaries.

Compared to CeFi, DeFi has the following pros and cons:

Pros:

- Anonymity – unlike CeFi, no KYC is required. Thus, borrowers remain anonymous and hence their privacy is protected from third-party issues
- No user biases - as the system relies on an algorithm to issue loans
- Automated – unlike CeFi that requires intermediaries, no need for human intervention is required in the issuance process. Thus, it is possible to issue instant loans
- High transparency – DeFi protocols and transactions are open for public view. Unlike CeFi, there are no secrets concerning loan issuance rules and protocols

Cons:

- Not beginner-friendly – unlike CeFi that has a human interface, newbies on DeFi will find it hard to get help. As such, they might not be able to maximize benefits from the platform.
- Comparatively riskier – compared to CeFi, DeFi lending platforms have a higher risk exposure due to a lack of KYC and AML rules.

Where to Get an NFT-backed Loan

DeFi is expanding exponentially. As such, the number of DeFi lending platforms continues to grow at a faster pace compared to CeFi lending platforms.

Popular DeFi crypto lending platforms include:

- Nexo
- Uniswap
- Maker

HOW TO INVEST IN NFT CRYPTO LENDING

You can invest in an NFT crypto lending business and thus earn income in addition to the potential capital gains. You don't have to let your crypto assets lie idle when they can generate for your passive income.

Most DeFi platforms allow NFT-collateralized crypto lending. It is now becoming more of an exception than a norm for a DeFi not to provide NFT-backed crypto lending.

The following are the main steps involved in NFT lending:

1. **Choose the right platform**

First of all, you have to decide whether you want to use the CeFi exchange (CEX) platform or the DeFi exchange (DEX) platform. If you are new to crypto lending, CeFi is more beginner-friendly. However, when it comes to employing NFT as collateral, the choice is largely limited to DeFi.

2. **Have the right loan product**

Some loan products only allow you to receive fiat currency against your collateral. Others allow you to receive cryptocurrency in addition to fiat currency. Yet, like all loan products, interest rate matters. As an investor, you would like to earn the highest possible interest rate. However, if you are a borrower, you would like to be charged the lowest possible interest rate. But, don't forget that interest is a factor of risk. Unlike traditional collateral where only lenders are exposed to risk, in the crypto world, even borrowers are also exposed to risk. Thus, it is important to consider the risk exposure of your crypto assets as collateral.

FACTORS TO CONSIDER WHILE SEEKING AN NFT-BACKED LOAN

When seeking a crypto loan an amalgamation of factors comes into play. You must not rely on just one or two factors but a balance of several factors to decide on whether to take up the crypto loan being offered or not.

The following are key factors ranked in their order of priority:

1. **The platform reputation**

Due to the high risk of hacking and platforms collapsing, it is important to consider mature platforms that have stood the test of time. How long the platform has been operating, the volume of transactions, security features, hacking history (thwarted hacking attempts, successful hacks, remedial action after successful hacking, etc.), and reviews (you should consider industry review, independent professional reviews, and customer reviews) are important reputational parameters to consider.

2. **Disclosure requirements**

Whether the platform has KYC and AML requirements and to what extent that exposes your privacy. While KYC and AML requirements help fish out bad actors, excessive KYC and AML requirements can breach your privacy and endanger your digital assets beyond the platform.

3. **Collateral requirement**

The collateral-to-loan (C2L) ratio is important. Some platforms require a 1:1 ratio, while others require a 2:1 ratio. The higher the ratio, the more your crypto assets are locked up and hence more exposed to the risk of hacking.

4. **Liquidity**

Some platforms have low liquidity, which means that it is harder to get loans. Those platforms with high liquidity mean that it is easier to get loans.

5. **The interest rate**

The interest rate is the actual cost of your loan. The higher the interest rate, the more expensive is your loan.

HOW TO ACQUIRE AN NFT-BACKED LOAN

While each NFT lending platform may have its own unique loan acquisition procedure, the following are the general procedures applicable to most platforms:

1. **Register with your preferred NFT lending platform**

The first step is to register with your preferred crypto lending platform so that you can open an account.

In the registration process, you will need to:

- Verify your identity
- Verify your collateral
- Provide other details and take other actions as may be needed

After this, some platforms may assign you a 'trust score' based on the assessment of your verification and compliance.

Upon successful registration, you will be provided with an account where you can transact on the platform.

2. **Select a loan product**

Once your account is active, the next logical step is to scout for your desired loan product. Your desired loan product will depend on:

- Collateral requirement
- Interest charges
- Other factors

After choosing your loan product, you submit your application for a loan using the platform's prescribed application form.

On successful submission of your loan application, you will start receiving loan offers from lenders.

3. **Accept offer**

Compare the various offers. Select the best offer. Accept it.

4. **Receive the loan**

Upon acceptance of the best offer, you will get the money almost instantly to your account.

PROS AND CONS OF NFT LENDING

NFT lending is a mixed bag of pros and cons. It is important to appreciate them so that when you are participating in them you can fathom your costs and gains.

PROS

- More accessible: Compared to banks, crypto lending is more accessible. This is because you don't need a bank account, credit score, and such complex registration and evaluation criteria to be allowed to borrow. Some crypto lending platforms (especially the DeFi lending platforms) are completely anonymous such that you don't need to comply with KYC (Know-your-customer) or AML (anti-money-laundering) requirements.
- Superfast: Very fast approval speed. Typically, loan approval happens within 24 hours.
- Customizable: Loan terms can be easily customized to fit the lender's requirements. Also, both the lender and borrower can mutually agree on terms.
- Safer than P2P: Due to KYC and AML restrictions, many lenders and borrowers resort to P2P lending platforms. However, P2P lending is not backed up by any collateral. Crypto loans are backed up by crypto assets.

Cons

- Extreme volatility: cryptocurrencies are highly volatile as their value fluctuates very fast and at big margins.
- Restricted fiat-crypto-fiat conversion: very few payment gateways allow one to convert fiat to crypto and vice versa. Most of those that do either limit the amount of crypto that can be converted (typically less than 2 bitcoins) or require stringent KYC and AML requirements.
- High collateral requirement: due to extreme volatility, it is typical to find a collateral requirement that is twice the value of the loan being advanced.
- High-security risk: crypto lending platforms are highly susceptible to hacking. Thus, the risk of losing crypto assets is significantly high

DeFi NFT Staking

Staking is the process of holding or locking crypto assets for purposes of future rewards or influence. As many blockchain networks shift away from proof-of-work (PoW) towards proof-of-stake (PoS), staking continues to gain relevance and importance.

Let's explore the two primary motivators for staking: rewards -vs- influence.

Staking for Rewards

The reward for staking is a monetary gain usually fixed at a percentage per year – just like a normal bank interest rate.

STAKING FOR INFLUENCE

Under the PoS, stakeholders vote based on their stakes to influence decisions regarding the direction that the network is going to take. Thus, the more stakes you have the greater is your influence. Staking for influence could also be termed as 'staking for power' (that is, the power to decide).

STAKING POOL

To leverage the power of collective bargaining, stakeholders can put their stakes into a collective pool. This pool will be considered as one unit. As we have already seen, the higher the stakes the greater the influence. As such, a stake pool has greater leverage when it comes to negotiating better terms – especially reward terms. Some networks allow a stake pool to decide as a single entity, though rare.

POPULAR CRYPTOS FOR DEFI STAKING

Not all cryptos can be staked. The following are the popular types of cryptos for staking:

- Tezos
- Algorand
- Synthetix
- DASH
- NEO
- LOOM
- Komodo

- QTUM
- Decred
- ICON
- ZCoin
- Cosmos (ATOM)
- PIVX
- NOW token
- Neblio
- OKCASH
- Stratis
- NAV Coin
- ETH 2.0
- Cardano

SPECIALIZED DeFi STAKING PLATFORMS

Specialized DeFi staking platforms exist to provide staking services for DeFi products. The following are the most popular DeFi staking platforms:

- Sythetix (SNX) – This platform provides synthetic assets (synths). Synths are virtual assets that act like derivatives for physical assets (such as gold) and real assets such as stocks, fiat currency, and even cryptos such as bitcoin. The native currency on this platform is SNX.
- Compound (COMP) – lenders and borrowers can interact on Compound to exchange established cryptocurrencies such as ETH, BAT, DAI, USDC, etc., at an interest. The platform employs liquidity pools where borrowers are required to deposit a certain sum of supported coins.
- Maker (MKR) – This platform allows users to leverage their stable coins against unstable coins such as bitcoin. The main stable coin used on this network is DAI. Therefore, lenders deposit DAI on the platform, which is

then lent to borrowers at a given interest. The borrowers deposit unstable coins as collateral.
- Yearn Finance (YFI) – This is a DeFi aggregator that distributes deposited funds into platforms that have the highest yield at the lowest risk. Thus, this aggregator strikes an optimal balance between yield and risk.

NATIVE NFT COINS FOR DIRECT STAKING
- Chiliz (CHZ)
- Decentraland (MANA)
- Theta (THETA)
- APENFT

BLOCKCHAIN NETWORKS THAT ALLOW NFT STAKING
- ETH 2.0
- Tron (TRON)
- Binance Smart Chain (BTCB)
- Tezos (XTZ)
- Polkadot (DOT)

STAKING NFT DERIVATIVES

In the literal sense, a derivative is simply an entity/item that has acquired properties of another entity/item. As such, a derivative is not independent of the main entity from which it has acquired the properties.

In the financial sense, a derivative is a financial security whose worth is dependent upon an underlying asset/security. For example, we do have gold derivatives, oil derivatives, stock derivatives, bond derivatives, etc.

It is common to have intangible derivatives of a tangible asset. This helps to facilitate trade in the tangible asset without the inconvenience of actually moving that tangible asset from one possession to the next. For example, it is extremely risky and cumbersome to keep moving gold from one place to another. Due to the high net worth of gold, it would be easy to trade in smaller units of it than the whole of it. Thus, one can buy and sell part-ownership of this gold in the form of a derivative. In this case, a derivative can be a simple as a certificate of part-ownership. However, it goes beyond this as some gold derivatives are pegged to the value of a goldmine, a gold mining company, or even a gold-trading company.

Bitcoin is the "gold standard" of cryptocurrency. Thus, just like gold derivatives, we can have bitcoin derivatives. And just as bitcoin derivatives, we can have derivatives of other cryptocurrencies and crypto-assets such as NFTs. Extrapolating this, we can then have stake derivatives.

Thus, staking a derivative is simply having a stake in a derivative of a given crypto asset or crypto-asset pool.

Derivatives make it easy to quantify assets, trade in them, and more importantly, diversify a portfolio. Derivatives also make it easy for one to blend different kinds of securities and trade in the units of this blend. For example, you can have a derivative from a blend of bitcoin and gold, cryptocurrency and NFTs, etc.

NFT STAKING PLATFORMS

- Cargo NFT
- Kraken Flow
- KingSWAP
- Superfarm
- Bondly
- OVR AI
- RAINI
- KIRA
- WAX (World Asset eXchange) NFT
- R-PLANET

NFTs STAKING EXCHANGE (NFT STEX) PLATFORMS

These are less specialized compared to StaaS. They mainly deal with the trading part of the coins/tokens. Thus, you can buy the coins/tokens from these exchanges and either stake them on the exchange or elsewhere.

The following are the most popular NFT STEX:

- Binance
- Coinbase

- KuCoin
- Kraken
- Poloniex

STAKING-AS-A-SERVICE (STAAS)

Due to the rise of PoS networks and the staking niche, specialized services for this market segment have come about. This makes it easy for stakeholders or potential stakeholders to receive quality service and thus gain maximum benefit from their stakes. Staking-as-a-service (StaaS) is the new name that blends a collection of various staking services as a package. The number of StaaS providers continues to rise as more crypto investors gain interest in the staking business. Some StaaS providers have established their own platforms for making this work easier.

DEFI STAAS

Specialized StaaS platforms have emerged to take care of the emerging and increasingly popular staking business. They offer more than what a general exchange platform offers. These are especially beginner-friendly for those who desire to engage in staking for the first time.

The following is a list of the most popular StaaS platforms:

- Figment networks
- MyContainer
- Stake Capital

- Stake.Fish
- Staked
- Stakinglab
- Staking Facilities
- Stakewith.us
- P2P Validator
- Dokia Capital

Using NFT to Provide Liquidity for DEX

Liquidity is what oils the financial machinery. For DEX, as financial machinery, to function effectively, it must be oiled by high liquidity. Liquidity, in financial terms, simply refers to the ability for cash and cash equivalents to flow from one point to another.

Fiat currency is cash, and cryptocurrency is its equivalent. For an exchange to easily take place on a DEX platform, it simply means cash and cash equivalents should be available and easily accessible as and when demanded.

However, unlike fiat currency that you can easily find in a bank and which a bank can easily order from the central bank (to print, if not available), cryptocurrencies are not available in unlimited quantity. As such, there has to be a sort of a way to incentivize holders of currency to release them into the market, in this case, the DEX.

How does DEX achieve this liquidity? Through liquidity pools...

LIQUIDITY POOL

A liquidity pool is simply a virtual collection of funds consolidated via locked-in smart contracts. In conventional banking, liquidity pools are easy to create due to the low costs of transaction fees. However, when it comes to cryptocurrency, the transaction fee cost makes it hard to harness liquidity. For example, in the centralized exchange (CEX), a central order book is maintained with a matching engine being able to match various orders.

In a fiat system, this CEX is maintained by the central bank, and orders are placed by banks. However, in the DEX system, there is no central entity that holding the cash assets. Rather, the assets are held by hundreds, thousands, or even millions of entities.

To overcome the complexity of having many holders of funds rather than a single entity as in the CEX system, DEX creates a liquidity pool through Automated Market Makers (AMM). Liquidity providers simply lock their funds in specialized crypto wallets, and AMM links them up to create a virtual pool. This virtual pool acts in the same way as a central bank. However, unlike the central bank, there is no physical pool. The virtual pool is simply a sum of locked-in funds in various smart contracts (wallets).

Thus, when someone borrows from the DEX liquidity pool (virtual pool), the person is, in effect, borrowing from many liquidity providers. The borrower receives from each liquidity provider an amount equivalent to the ratio of the provider's contribution into the pool. Hence, the liquidity provider will earn a portion of interest from the borrowed fund equivalent to his/her ratio of contribution to the pool.

Yet, unlike the central bank, which, by law, can demand a certain amount to be deposited into its reserve account and can also order a certain amount of currency to be printed to fill the reserve account, DEX has no such luxury. As such, DEX incentivizes liquidity holders to lock their funds into the liquidity pools for a certain period. Interest and other kinds of benefits are offered to liquidity providers for doing so.

Chapter 11

The Future of NFTs

What does the future hold for NFTs?

Well, NFTs, though still at the infancy stage, are here to stay. The horizon of imagination about NFT's potential use-cases stretches deeper into the future.

However, certain things have to happen as this novel concept evolves into maturity. Some interventions by stakeholders have to be made. But the bulk of the changes are a natural path of evolution as the technology matures.

More RV-based NFTS coming aboard, specialized NFT exchanges, expanded use-cases, wider adoption, market stabilization, improved standardization, minimizing scams, and going mainstream are some of the markers that will shape the future direction of NFTs as they establish a strong foothold in the world of crypto assets. We are going to discuss each of these markers, albeit briefly.

A GRADUAL SHIFT FROM SV-BASED NFTS TO RV-BASED NFTS

Currently, most NFTs hold sentimental value (SV). As such, their worth is in the minds of those who buy them. They obey the maxim that "beauty is in the eyes of the beholder." The SV-NFTs have no standard value. This makes it hard for them to be easily tradeable and exchangeable as their value is subject to the hype, sentiments, speculation, and change in taste. This has no problem at all since it is the nature of art.

On the other hand, NFTs that hold real value (RV) are less sentimental, less susceptible to hype and speculation. Their worth is determined by the real value of the underlying property. For example, an NFT that represents a land title or gold holding is more likely going to be stable in value. Someone holding such an NFT expects the value to remain relatively stable in the future. It is the RV-NFTs that are more likely going to dominate the future as their use-cases are more and easier to integrate into the e-commerce world.

RV-NFTs are likely going to go mainstream and easily adopted than SV-NFTs. All that is required is a change in laws to recognize them. If the law recognizes the use of digital signatures, digital currencies (digitized fiat currencies), and digital records, it is quite easy for the same law to recognize RV-NFTs. Just as Bitcoin has been gradually receiving legal recognition by the fiat-based bureaucracies, RV-NFTs are going to gradually receive similar recognition.

MORE SPECIALIZED NFT EXCHANGES

So far, a few exchanges have established a niche as NFT marketplaces. However, most of them are differentiated branches of the same tree – Ethereum. While Ethereum holds a stranglehold on smart contracts and by extension NFTs and DeFi, there is a need for more blockchain networks to come about, especially those that will be more specialized on NFT.

The main disadvantage of the near-monopoly by Ethereum network in as far as NFTs and their DeFi sister are concerned is the mining/minting and transaction costs. Gas is still very expensive and thus discourages day-to-day NFT use-cases that would require very low pricing.

There is future potential for more NFT and DeFi ecosystems that offer efficient and cost-effective alternatives to Ethereum. We have so far mentioned eight of them (excluding BSC) that provide minting tokens, but their current share of NFT minting is quite minimal. Their growth and expansion will bring competition and further improvisation on the backbone technology, thus giving consumers better prices and investors/traders better returns.

MORE NFT BLOCKCHAIN NETWORKS

Initially, the Ethereum network was the only blockchain network where NFTs could be possibly mined due to the ERC-721 standard. Right now, there are eight recognized competitors that we have already mention, including Tron, among others. As NFTs use-cases expand and demand increase, more NFT blockchain networks will crop up that will offer an alternative solution to Ethereum's strangulating bottlenecks.

REDUCED COST OF MINTING NFTS

The high cost of minting NFTs on the Ethereum network has prompted competitors to spring up. Greater competition means the lowered cost of minting. Eventually, the Ethereum network will be forced to find more economical and competitive ways to stay afloat. Already, due to the high cost of PoW, Ethereum is transitioning to PoS. Other networks are already transitioning to dPoS, which is cheaper than PoS. DeFi staking is already an alternative way of dealing with crypto assets without the expensive mining process. IDO (Initial DEX Offering), is gaining rapid acceptance as a better and cheaper alternative to the expensive mining-based ICO (Initial Coin Offering).

The more the cost of minting goes down, the wider will be the RV-NFT adoption. RV-NFTs can only be viable if the margin between the value of the underlying real asset and that of the token is minimal; otherwise, it won't make sense to tokenize such real assets.

EXPANDED USE-CASES

So far, NFTs have not broken into the world of real business. They are still scratching the surface of the world of arts.

The vast world of real estate awaits NFTs' maturity. I foresee NFT being the future of certifications when it comes to international trade, insurance, e-commerce, notaries, and many more.

DEEPER NFT-DEFI INTEGRATION

NFT started as a crypto art. However, the recent trends show that it is etching out a niche in the fintech sector. As more financial instruments become tokenized, NFT gets deeper into the DeFi world. Already, we do have NFT promissory notes. The promissory notes are a precursor to NFT security instruments.

WIDER ADOPTION

So far, despite the hype, NFTs are still not yet widely adopted. However, with the speed with which NFTs are grabbing territory from other crypto assets and the traditional assets, the sky is still not the limit.

As the hype dust settles, business executives and government functionaries who are often fence-sitters when it comes to emerging technologies will start stepping into the NFT field, albeit cautiously. Bitcoin took almost a decade before starting to gain a warm embrace by the officialdom. So far, no world government has fully embraced Bitcoin and other cryptocurrency networks. There is still a lukewarm reception despite cryptocurrencies staking almost $2 trillion of the global economy – almost displacing the entire 1.4 billion-people Indian economy.

There is a lot of hope. Unlike fully virtual cryptocurrencies, NFT has real-world use-cases that are likely to fasten the wider adoption.

MARKET STABILIZATION

So far, NFTs have remained more of a hype. Not until a trend is established such that prices are stable, for most of the NFTs, market stabilization will take some time. This will depend on the adoption by business entities, institutional entities, and government entities where RV-NFTs will represent real properties rather than mere artistic hype.

Improved Standardization

While ERC-721 and ERC-1155 are the current standards, there are still lots of loose ends to tighten up. This is understandable given that NFT is a novel idea and still at the exploratory stages despite the exponential explosion.

Standards will improve as the NFTs mature. With wider adoption, more players will demand better rules and protocols and also contribute their knowledge in their respective fields such as insurance, notary, clearing and forwarding, real estate registry, among others.

Minimizing scams

Currently, the rate of scamming is still high as far as NFTs are concerned. Through improved standardization, the rate of scams will go down as bad players will find themselves being weeded out. The advantage of blockchain is that it has a sophisticated mechanism of weeding out scams based on their amply documented history.

Marketplaces such as SuperRare and Nifty Gateway, have employed very strict verification and authentication mechanism that establishes genuine players and valid NFT assets. As more similar marketplaces come about, players will have an option of whether to go for the extremely secure marketplaces that have a high-security barrier to entry or those with a low-security barrier to entry but more insecure. At least players will have informed choices.

GOING MAINSTREAM

Going mainstream means that NFTs become a normal part of the transactional process rather than a hype still residing in the novel world. The year 2021 has marked the NFTs' baby steps into the mainstream world.

Succeeding mainstream will depend on how various industry players, government agencies, and other institutional entities adopt the NFTs. Furthermore, it will also depend on the effort undertaken by respective blockchain networks and trading platforms in streamlining the NFT generation and marketing process. Finally, this will also depend on how the respective blockchain networks and trading platforms go about reducing transactional costs. As of now, the transaction cost per NFT is still very high, which inhibits the adoption of RV-NFT applicable to most of the day-to-day transactional use-cases such as eCommerce.

Addressing NFT challenges

NFT is not without challenges. There are myriad challenges, including legal, financial, and technical challenges. However, they are not insurmountable. Addressing these challenges is part and parcel of NFT growth and maturity.

Legal challenges

Legal challenges largely emanate from copyrights, patents, and enforcement of rights in a Court of law in the absence of Statutes governing NFT.

While some marketplaces have put up strict verification and authentication procedures, the bulk of the marketplaces are awash with NFT minted out of artworks whose intellectual property rights have been infringed.

Since buying a stolen property does not confer ownership and holding a stolen property is criminal in many jurisdictions, NFT derived from such stolen property becomes dubious and legally unenforceable.

NFT AND INTELLECTUAL PROPERTY RIGHTS (NFT-IPR)

It is no doubt intellectual property (IP) issues arise when it comes to NFT. It is not just about the legal challenges already mentioned but how the IP is assigned, distributed, and managed.

NFT DIGITAL RIGHTS MANAGEMENT (NFT DRM)

One big advantage of NFT is that you don't have to sell your NFT asset/property. You can simply sell the access rights (e.g., to access NFT content and read/listen to), display rights (e.g., the right to display a piece of artwork in a particular gallery).

Thus, non-fungibility does not limit selling the property to multiple buyers. You can create different rights and monetize each right without foregoing the ownership. That is the beauty of NFT.

However, NFT DRM is only as good as the legality of the asset itself. While NFT DRM makes the work of assigning and distributing rights easy, fast and cost-effective, it is still hampered by the IP challenges already mentioned.

TECHNICAL CHALLENGES

Rug-pull is still a technical challenge. Ensuring that the embedded URL in the NFT that points to the location where the digital asset is hosted remains technically unfeasible. If the host collapses or winds up, then the asset being referenced by the NFT is lost. While IPFS (Interplanetary File System) is considered more reliable and the best option so far, it can also be susceptible to flaws.

CONCLUSION

Thank you for acquiring this book and reading it to this point.

This book has not only introduced you to the world of NFTs but also the world of blockchain and cryptocurrencies.

I hope that you have found this book a valuable companion and a worthy investment. I also, hope that you have been inspired enough to create your own NFTs and leveraged your NFTs to gain profit and other benefits.

This is the moment to share your inspiration with others by encouraging them to acquire a copy of this book so that they too can come aboard. Encourage them to join the blockchain revolution and book an NFT ticked to the world of creativity and fortunes.

Again, thank you for purchasing this book and furnishing your mind with endless gems of new digital opportunities.

Good Luck!

www.ingramcontent.com/pod-product-compliance
Lightning Source LLC
Chambersburg PA
CBHW060826220526
45466CB00003B/996